BRIGHTER SIDE OF THE BROOM

By Don Aslett
America's #1 Cleaning Expert

The Brighter Side of the Broom

Published by:

Marsh Creek Press
PO Box 700
Pocatello, Idaho 83204
Phone 208-232-3535
Fax 208-235-5481
www.aslett.com

ISBN 0-937750-34-4

To purchase this book in quantity at a discount,
contact the publisher above.

Editor: Carol Cartaino
Production manager: Tobi Alexander
Illustrator: David Lock
Graphic design: Ryan Roghaar

More Books by Don Aslett

Books on decluttering and personal organization:

Clutter's Last Stand
For Packrats Only
Clutter Free! Finally & Forever
The Office Clutter Cure
Weekend Makeover (Lose 200 Lbs. This Weekend)
DONE! (How to Have a 48-Hour Day)
How to Handle 1,000 Things at Once
Dejunk Live! (Audio CD)

Other books on home care:

HELP! Around the House
No Time to Clean!
Is There Life After Housework?
Do I Dust or Vacuum First?
The Cleaning Encyclopedia
Don Aslett's Clean in a Minute
Don Aslett's Stainbuster's Bible
Make Your House Do the Housework
Who Says It's a Woman's Job to Clean?
Wood Floor Care
Pet Clean-Up Made Easy
Painting Without Fainting

Autobiography:

How I Swept My Way to the Top: The Don Aslett Story

Business books:

Barnyard to Boardroom: Business Basics
DONE! (How to Have a 48-Hour Day)
The Office Clutter Cure
Keeping Work Simple (with Carol Cartaino)
How to Be #1 With Your Boss
Speak Up! A Step-by-Step Guide to Powerful Public Speeches
A Toilet Cleaner's Attitude

For professional cleaners:

Cleaning Up for a Living
The Professional Cleaner's Personal Handbook
How to Upgrade & Motivate Your Cleaning Crews
Construction Cleanup
Professional Cleaner's Clip Art

Other:

How Successful People Keep Their Lives Out of the Toilet (with Sandra Phillips)

Writing books:

Get Organized, Get Published! (with Carol Cartaino)
How to Write and Sell Your First Book
You Can... You Should... Write Poetry

About the Author

Don Aslett has made himself the national spokesperson for "clean," and perhaps the biggest secret of the overwhelming success of his books and speeches is the down-to-earth humor he brings to every subject.

This volume brings together the best of Don's "funny cleaning stories"—the accounts of wild and woolly happenings on the job that have delighted fans and audiences everywhere over the years.

Don Aslett committed himself to his profession at an early age, in grade school and on the family ranch, when he determined life was better and you were treated better when things were clean and in order. To earn his way through college he organized a cleaning company and turned a "get by" job into a lifelong career. His company—Varsity Contractors—today operates throughout the U.S. and Canada and is a leader in the industry.

Don has written more than three dozen books, many of them bestsellers, and made more than 10,000 media and speaking appearances. He has a thriving mail-order and retail cleaning supplies business, as well as a company that designs homes and devices that make everyday life easier, and he is now building the world's largest cleaning museum. At 72 he's still actively dedicated to a "day's work" in the profession.

Don and his wife, Barbara, have been married for 50 years. They have six children, 18 grandchildren, and two great-grandchildren. They divide their time between their ranch in Southern Idaho and their maintenance-free home in Kauai, Hawaii.

Contents

Introduction

For more than half a century now I've been a toilet cleaner, floor cleaner, a "cleaning man." One of the most shunned, dreaded, and lowest paid professions around is the one I picked more than 50 years ago and the one I'm still in, an industry most consider the last resort, the least rewarding and for sure the one with just about the lowest image. And what a great choice it was!!!

I'm a janitor—if you wince at that word you have permission to call me a custodian. "Sanitation engineer" is okay, too, if you insist. I'm a professional cleaner, who cleans up after people and the world. I got started in this business at age nineteen while a freshman at Idaho State University, and have stuck to it and made a million dollars, in fact many millions, mopping floors, cleaning windows and toilets and all the rest. My business now has thousands of employees, is nationally recognized, and has branched off into several other related businesses. I've also written more than three dozen books, sold almost four million copies of them, and made around 10,000 TV, radio, and speech presentations.

Cleaning, I soon discovered, is almost a guarantee of a satisfying and successful life, not a dull, end-of-the-road, meaningless, get-by job you take in desperation until something better comes along. It was a diamond in the rough just waiting to be polished. It not only made me wealthy and encouraged a healthy mind and body, but enabled me to make armies of friends and clients, find many good partners and colleagues, and influence the lives of others all over the world positively. And even all of this was nothing compared to the fun and exhilaration of actually *being* a janitor. I've enjoyed myself every minute!

Yes, with bowl cleaner and a broom, and those books I authored, there wasn't and still isn't anything dull or low-class about cleaning and maintenance.

A side note before you start...

If you were asked to write up a paragraph on your life, it would be fairly simple and give the reader just enough information to place you in history or in your family records. Your life summary would probably be in a format somewhat like mine:

> Don Aslett, raised on an Idaho farm, went to college and started a cleaning business to work his way through school. He hired fellow students to help, and built the business into a significant operation. He married and he and his wife had six children while still in college. After graduation he stayed in the cleaning industry as a career, expanding his company and becoming a national spokesperson for cleaning.

That would be the short version, the capsule. But your life, as mine, also has a long version, which contains the strains, struggles, and stumbles as well as the progress and productivity, peace and pleasures. There would be thousands of such incidents if you kept a daily journal to allow full and accurate recall of all the details that are missed in the short version of your life. Much of this detail, both the glitches and the good times, would have tremendous value if it were shared with not only friends and family and society in general, but with those directly in your industry. I happen to believe my profession of professional cleaner (which I have practiced for 50 years) has more challenges and comedy than any other, and have some proof in these pages from my journal records to validate that claim.

Your first reaction after reading this volume (if you don't run out immediately to take up a janitorial career) might be that you would never hire me or my Varsity crew to clean your house or building. Please keep these adventures in custodial duties in perspective as you read them, however, realizing that—because they're more unusual and funnier—I'm concentrating on the occasional reverses or boo-boos over those 50 years rather than describing everyday cleaning chores. There were far more congratulations than catastrophes on the job. I've just picked some of the oddest events out of my journal to share with you.

Millions of us clean for a living—I believe we are the world's biggest profession. There is all kinds of moving and shaking going on in this business, fresh adventure with every shift. Humor and quirks of human nature abound in every house, office building, mall, parking lot, and bank we service. I've met all kinds of interesting people in all kinds of places, gaining exposure and education I'd challenge anyone in any other profession to equal.

This collection of some of the all-in-a-day's work experiences on the job will warm your heart and raise your opinion of those of us who come behind you each day and night to clean and care for the buildings you use. My cleaning company, Varsity Contractors, has grown to be a huge, premium operation despite some of the graceless, even bungling things that occurred along the way. Those goofs, surprises, and reverses actually helped to develop and refine what is today a sophisticated and well-run corporation. We survived and eventually thrived, and believe it or not, the customers did too!

Get ready to go on and enjoy some cleaning jobs with me and my crews. Some of this might seem unbelievable, but it's all true! It's been a trip, in more than a half-century on the job, and all of the following stories happened somewhere along the way.

Don Aslett

Chairman of the Board
Varsity Contractors, Inc.

CHAPTER 1

The Early Days

New blood in an old profession

O R YOU might say, a new approach to an old profession. Cleaning is a necessity—the need for it has been here since the day the Lord put Adam in the garden and told him to "take care" of it. The Roman god Janus (for whom not just janitors but the month of January was named) was custodian of the empire's treasure and from then right on into the twenty-first century some version of the custodian or janitor has always been around to clean up messes.

Performing this service not as an employee but as a contractor was almost a revolution and a tough sales job, as I was one of the first in not just my city but my part of the country and the world to approach it this way in some areas of business. The cleaning itself was often quite an adventure, too, because there were few instruction manuals on the subject around back in the 1950s, only the labels of the wax and soap containers and a few old USDA bulletins, so I had to take it from there. So don't be too critical of, or shocked by some of the events during those first years of my professional cleaning company.

Cool, clear... water?

Be careful what you put in old containers. Make sure that anything you put in a can or bottle is clearly and accurately marked—the minute you put it in there.

People have often asked me why I became a janitor, and when I think back to my childhood, there was one experience that could have played a part. I was twelve, and at this impressionable age had joined a new Scout troop, #99, and after two meetings, there wasn't a more dedicated or industrious Scout. Because there wasn't much else going on in our quiet, isolated Idaho farm community in 1946, Scouting received my full attention.

At the third meeting, our Scoutmaster announced a coming hike. I had never been on an official hike in my life, and after reading the Scout manual and looking at the pictures of uniformed boys on the trail, I couldn't wait for the day. We were given a list of things that we would need for the hike, including a canteen to supply the necessary drinking water, especially since we were hiking in the desert of Southern Idaho. The official Scout canteen I saw in the book was not within my budget of 60 cents, so following my father's example of making whatever he needed, but didn't have or couldn't afford, I decided to make a canteen.

Searching through Mom's cupboards, I came upon the perfect container: a flat, quart-sized metal can of Aero wax. Shaking it, I found only a dribble of wax in the bottom and so was granted permission to have it. I rinsed it out until the water was clean and clear. (Of course I didn't know that cold water wouldn't dissolve the layer of hardened wax that had built up on the inside of the can over time.) I then made an insulated and padded cover for it from a piece of old Army blanket, stitching it up nicely with some thick black thread. It was a beaut! After I added a belt loop and carrying strap to it, I was prepared!

The morning of the hike I didn't drink anything before I left home because I wanted to be sure to get as much use out of the canteen as I could. Out into the desert we went, a long line of Boy Scouts. My gurgling canteen at my side gave me great pride and confidence. By 10 A.M. it was hot and my mouth felt like cotton when we stopped to rest. My first big draft of cool, clear water was not as thrilling as I expected. The heat and slogging had loosened about a cup of old wax that I had failed to clean out of the canteen, and thus what I drank was... diluted wax. It was terrible, and now my mouth tasted like waxed cotton. I wanted desperately to ask a fellow Scout for a drink of water so I wouldn't gag, but I had bragged so much about my homemade canteen being better than their boughten ones that I didn't have the nerve. On we went, my reservoir of wax sloshing at my side and me belching wax. For lunch, I'd brought one of my dad's famous cheese and egg sandwiches and two of Mom's peanut butter ones for energy—two of the driest sandwiches you could eat. Trying to wash them down with wax water was tough.

By 3 P.M., we were in one of the highest, driest spots on earth. I could spit dust, and had only my can of wax to drink. As the desert heat waves danced across the horizon, I could only stagger along, feeling like I'd just licked a few thousand square feet of kitchen linoleum. In a desperate attempt to rid myself of

the wax so that I could graciously accept a drink from some-one else, I "accidentally" knocked over my canteen. But before more than a few drops of the liquid had trickled out, an alert Scout nearby leaped up and snatched it up, saving my "water" (which he bragged about all the way home).

That evening coming home, when we walked past a canal of muddy water, my whole soul said, "Dive in and drink." The canal ran through a corral of several thousand cows, but that wasn't why I didn't do it. It was saving face.

By the end of the day, floor wax was surely in my system and has been ever since!

The birth of a cleaning company

Don't expect the world to beat a path to your door, especially when you're just starting out. One notice of your existence is never enough!

After I decided to start a little cleaning business to help pay my way through college, I convinced my roommates to join me and put an ad in the paper. I picked the name Varsity House-cleaners (later changed to Varsity Contractors) and put an ad in the paper—"Don Aslett—Professional Cleaner" (I'd hardly ever made my bed up till now). The landlady of our off-campus dorm room agreed for a percentage to take any calls and we were in business. We passed our cards out all over town and went home to discuss what we were going to do with all of our money. I trembled all day in school anticipating the beginning of our very own operation and rushed home after my last lab. I'd envisioned a page full of calls from people begging us to rescue them from all sorts of dirty situations, but there was only one… "to clean around a furnace." Disappointed, I put on my new coveralls and scampered up the street to do the job.

When I arrived at the address, my vision of greatness was restored. The house was a mansion, one of the finest in town. A classy, attractive woman answered the door and then led me downstairs to the furnace room. She pointed to a narrow space between the furnace hopper and the coal bin. "The coal has fallen in that crack for years and is a fire hazard. Can you get it out of such a tight spot?" "What a snap," I thought as I assured her that her troubles were over. "How much do you charge?" she said. It took all of my nerve to blurt out the staggering fee of $1.25 an hour we had decided on. She squinted at me and finally said, "Well… okay." Then she left and I tore into the job, quickly devising a way to get the accumulated coal out of its unwelcome resting place. I then dusted and cleaned the whole area in record time and called for the lady of the house to come down and inspect my job. "Oh my," she said, "that's beautiful work!" Glancing at her watch, she then said, "Let's see, you've been here for 56 minutes… at $1.25 an hour." She pulled out a pad and did logarithms and long division for a few minutes and then said, "That comes to exactly $1.18." She counted out the change with a smile. "You're a good worker and I'll call you again."

I could hardly believe what I had just experienced. I'd expected a little more than the hourly rate for doing that three-hour job in less than un hour. As I turned in the takings of our first day in business and recounted the story, we decided business was tougher than it appeared.

This woman did call me again to weed her garden and I assured her my experience in horticulture was second to none so her garden was in good hands. I still think that expensive African Droop-a-Doodle I cut down looked just like a cocklebur, and in any case that was the last time she called me.

Others in the city began to call, however, and by then I had learned a few marketing maneuvers. I took one of our cards over to the college switchboard and told the young woman there to give this number to anyone calling for cleaning or yard work. She did and the work began to roll in.

Beginner's pluck

Mistakes are inevitable, in work and in life—failing to learn from them is the only unforgivable mistake.

Being a farm boy, I was willing to tackle anything. After all, I'd been cleaning up after pigs and cows for years.

One day a woman called and said she wanted her carpet shampooed. I had never seen a carpet. On the farm we had old linoleum floors and an outdoor toilet.

I ran downtown and rented a rug machine, read the little manual that came with it, put a uniform on, and showed up at the woman's house with all of my equipment. The woman was really impressed. The only thing I could remember Mother doing when she was cleaning was using really hot water. This woman had a big, thick wool carpet and when I finished that job, she thought she had a throw rug. I shrank that carpet about four inches away from every wall.

Two days later, I was using lacquer thinner in a small sewing room, and the fumes did in the customer's pet parakeet. About a week later I was washing a ceiling with ammonia, and it dripped down some and I didn't wipe it up, so it left a big white spot on top of a grand piano. Gradually my reputation spread through the college city of Pocatello, and I did get better (at cleaning, not ruining). Every house I'd go to, the women would say, "Do it this way, Don," "Do it that way," "Try this." Soon I could do the work much faster and better.

Business boomed and bigger jobs rolled my way. One spring month my net income while going to school was an unbelievable $250. In those days many people working full time weren't making that much.

I hired one, two, three other students to help, then ten and twenty and later hundreds. Some of the students who joined me early on stayed with me over the years and became managers, and some would later be a great influence on my life and the company. Arlo Luke, for instance, was a pharmacy student my wife and I met on our honeymoon. Arlo was a clean-cut blonde, 5'8" tall and 150 pounds of dynamite. He was not one to take second place to anyone or anything. He's been with me almost 50 years now, and is CEO of Varsity. Likewise, Mark Browning, a handsome nineteen-year-old ISU student from Rigby, Idaho, was a plumber's son. Nineteen when he joined us, he was sharp, skilled in many things, and learned faster than others. Within months he was another of my leading men, and a great mentor (which he is to this day—now the President of Varsity).

The vision I had now of potential was unbelievable. It was hard work and not very glamorous, but you met a lot of interesting people and learned a lot. In fact, it was hard to beat!

Our first loser

A lesson that losses can happen in pursuit of gains, and that this bid business has to be worked out carefully!

Just as the snow was melting in March of 1958, the Grims School of Business, a college on the second floor of a big building downtown, called us to bid the cleaning of all twelve of their classrooms and a large hall. We bid $175 for the whole job. The president of the school, after looking over the bid, told us to "Get with it!" We were elated, so much so that my wife and I felt we could now afford our first car and bought a 1951 Chevy for $250. We drove home that weekend to crow a little to our parents about the gold mine we'd found.

When the job started, we knew we'd found a mine all right— a coal mine. We soon realized that we had grossly underbid the job. The paint on the 12-foot high ceilings was ancient water-based, almost unwashable, and the rooms seemed to have doubled in size since we bid them. The walls, which looked green, when cleaned, were really light pink—they were unbelievably dirty. We didn't have much experience with cleaning problems then, and it was a total disaster. We labored days in each room. We built scaffolding, tried putting the cleaning solution in weed sprayers, and everything else we could think of to speed the job up. In contractor's terms, we lost our shirts, making (after a month of labor between classes and on weekends) just a few pennies an hour. To make a long story about a long job short, we worked the last three 12-hour days for nothing. My hands were so ammonia-shrunk that when baseball practice started, the coach thought I had a white mitt on my pitching hand.

Cleaning the fast lane

One day, while washing walls in the small Chamber of Commerce office in downtown Pocatello, I met the Chamber President, a salesman deluxe. I started telling him our success story—six people going to school and learning the scientific approach to scrubbing toilets. His eyes got bigger than my exaggerations and finally he could contain himself no longer and rushed out the door. Minutes later he came back dragging the general manager of the famous Hotel Bannock, where Judy Garland was born in a trunk. It was a swanky, high-end place for the railroad town of Pocatello.

Mr. Chamber of Commerce introduced me as a superman who could clean anything. The hotel manager was impressed and within two days we had our first janitorial contract for $525 a month. This meant a steady income that we could depend on and so we hired a few more men. There was one small hitch, however—cleaning time didn't start until 11 P.M. at night and in the bar area not till 1 A.M. We usually finished cleaning before 3 A.M., if we worked really hard. And we worked hard—we ran.

The hotel job had a lot of value to Varsity as far as education went. I was innocent of the other side of life and was soon made to realize that it was somewhat different than I knew. I never had heard many women use profanity and judged all womankind by my lovely mother, grandmother, and wife. I trusted everyone, and took people at face value, I had never been around alcoholic beverages at all and the night hotel and bar crowds were an education in reality. Weirdos of all kinds, ladies of the night, hard drinkers, politicians and police on the take, cheating spouses, and many other things could be seen here or passing through.

My brother, Larry, worked for us for a while. He was an ingenious fellow, often pushing his cleaning equipment into the

bar at 1:05 A.M. to clean, squealing with delight as he snatched a five or ten-dollar bill from the formerly dark floor. This really stimulated the bar crew and as I reflect now, I wonder if ole' Larry planted the money just to motivate the late-hour cleaning crew.

One night, just fifteen minutes before the bar closed, I was vacuuming the lobby when a customer staggered out of the bar and wobbled toward me. "Which way to the restroom, buddy?" he slurred out. "Down the hall and to the left," I said. He grunted and weaved down the hall, turning right instead of left. He stumbled through the darkened dining room and burst through swinging doors into the kitchen. The sudden presence of lots of light, hard flooring, sinks, and plumbing pipes must have signaled, "bathroom." On the floor about urinal height was a large caldron of peeled potatoes soaking overnight in water. When I barged through the door to give the drunk new directions, he was peeing right into those good Idaho potatoes.

I reported this foul deed to the oversized, tattoo-armed night chef, who snorted, "Hell, just won't have to salt 'em, now." I avoided ordering potatoes at that hotel for three years, just to be on the safe side.

Another not so lovely experience was cleaning the grill hood vents at the restaurants and cafés that the Department of Health said to "clean up or close up." The owners were generally mad at the health officials and took it out on us as we skated and slid around in those grease-laden caverns, ammonia and "grease release" strippers running down our arms and necks. Most of the owners had enough mercy to close down the kitchen a day for the purpose, but some didn't, and scraping and scrubbing grease over the top of a hot stove and a fierce-looking 295-pound chef with a hangover was an experience indeed.

"Mommy, it's raining downstairs!"

Overselling can come back to bite you, so especially don't oversell anything not well tested by time!

How about some couldn't-believe-my-eyes carpet adventures? It was the late 50s, and what carpet cleaning expertise there was was self-taught. We had impressive machines that made plenty of noise as we sincerely sought to discover or invent procedures that would really do the job.

We finally had our own carpet cleaning machine, after renting one for months, and were doing more carpet cleaning every week. Carpeting was getting popular, prices were coming down, and many old hardwood floors were being covered with carpet.

On one job, a woman asked me to put some dye in with my shampoo. She said that it would perk up and brighten her rather dull carpet. I was hesitant, but it was her carpet and she said to do it, and assured me everything would be fine. So I added the dye and cleaned the rug. The result was beautiful—the dye had done just what she said it would. The carpet was not only clean but a fresh new green, and the dye hid some of the stains and wear. We added this bit of wisdom to our records and for the next month or so many homeowners were impressed as we shared our secret. (It was easy to do because my wife Barbara and I had bought our first house from a carpet dyer who left a big shelf of dye behind.) Our new "carpet rejuvenation" program came to a rather expensive end one dark day.

We answered a call to clean a carpet, and the lady of the house was one that even the most dashing entrepreneur would want to impress. "For two extra dollars, Ma'am, we will use super-snort dye additive to give this old carpet a lift." "No," she said. To a hungry young businessman, that means, "I don't understand—tell me again." So I asked again, and she said no three more times. Determined to impress her and show her I was right, I said, "Okay, I'll add it free!" "If you insist," she said, and I did.

I plugged the machine in, poured in the dye, and got busy on her carpet. I'd done scores of such jobs by now, but this one, when finished, just didn't look right. "Oh," she said, "look at my carpet!" It looked like a dead leopard. I was cool, having learned by now to sweat undetected, on the back of my neck instead of my forehead. "Don't worry, Ma'am, the hydro suds just barely penetrated the fiber flexers" (making it up as I went along). I refilled the shampoo tank and went over the rug again, but it was no better. I knew I was in trouble, plus she kept saying her truck driver husband would be home any minute and glancing at his TV chair, I saw a four-foot span between the seat cushion and where his greasy head hit the back of the chair—he must be 7'2"!

So I went for broke, and went over the carpet a third time with the shampoo release valve fully open. This transformed it from a dead leopard to a dead pinto horse. About then, up the stairs from the basement came her daughter, panicked—"Mommy, it's raining downstairs!" The river running out of my shampoo tank had fully saturated the carpet and was flowing down the heat vents and dripping off the ceiling in the basement. Needless to say I got out of there quick and the family got a new rug at my expense!

The people who replaced the carpet informed me later that her rug was a fiber blend, and the cotton had absorbed the dye while the rayon and nylon didn't. That was not the first or last carpet to give up its life in the course of my efforts to become a premier carpet cleaner.

None of us professional carpet cleaners in the old days could get all of the water out of carpets we were cleaning. When we were up against a really grungy bugger we had to really soak it down, and the wet/dry vacuums we used then got little of it back up. So the carpet stayed wet for days afterward and problems always followed. In one house, we forgot to block the legs of a piano and the steel casters rusted and stuck to the rug (besides warping the piano out of tune). In another house, the woman closed up all of the windows after one of these "wet" carpet jobs, trapping in the moisture. When I arrived the next morning after a raving phone call from her, there were long sheets of wallpaper draped all over the rug. I couldn't imagine who would sling wallpaper onto a wet rug, until I found out from the sobbing woman that the wallpaper came off the walls—all that moisture loosened the glue!

Carpet power

Extra-wet anything usually means trouble or damage potential, so be extra wary!

Another of our customers owned a rental house, and wanted the carpet cleaned before the next renters moved in. By now I was perhaps not the best at cleaning them, but I was getting pretty good at sniffing out potential problems. The empty living room was large, and on the floor was a thick woolen carpet. The former tenants had pets that peed all over it, so we knew a deep, wet suds cleaning would be required and shrinkage was likely to result, unless, my mechanical mind told me, the carpet was anchored to the floor with more than a wimpy tack strip. I had my utility truck with me and the smallest nails in it were 16 penny (more than 3 inches long). I used them to quickly nail the edges of the carpet to the wooden floor beneath. The heads of the giant nails were well hidden by the heavy nap. Then we really put the liquid to it—soaked, sudsed, and rinsed the carpet—and extracted as much as we could back out with a wet/dry vacuum. The carpet looked fine afterward, as we opened some windows to aid the drying process and left for another job.

About eight hours later we came back for a final check and were unable to believe what we saw. The strength of a shrinking wool carpet is incredible! It had pulled pieces of tongue and groove wood right out of the floor along the walls. There lay our clean carpet, five inches away from the wall, trimmed with upside-down 20-foot long boards with rows of 16-penny nails sticking out of them. I don't even want to remember how we remedied that one!

Cold carpet

*Putting anything anywhere "just for now" is a
good recipe for loss, damage, and confusion.*

Our operation got bigger and supervisors handled many jobs by themselves now. Arlo would run crews as my assistant manager and so would other men. To organize us better I constructed a large schedule board on which all jobs were placed under the date they were to be done. When the men arrived they simply picked up a card describing the job they were assigned and what vehicle to take and then packed up the equipment and went. This worked well and enabled us to run four and five jobs at the same time.

Some confusion occasionally occurred, of course, and minor disasters struck from time to time. Once, for instance, when I added some antifreeze to the truck, the container was leaking so I poured what was left over into the only container available around the shop, an empty rug shampoo bottle. Then I tucked it away where no one would find it. Someone did, however, and took it on a job. They were gone for hours and I questioned their late return. Both men were worn out and one said, "Man, that was tough. We got the rug clean eventually, but boy did we have trouble getting the shampoo to foam." This may have been the only antifreeze-cleaned carpet in the world. It, like our dye invention, was immediately eliminated from further use.

Signs of the trade

*Make sure the traces of your trade are ones you
don't mind carrying!*

Embarrassment, not from work, but as a result of it, was frequent as my business grew. I was elected Vice President of SNEA (the Student National Education Association) for the State of Idaho in my sophomore year, and was President-Elect the following year. As a sophomore, too, I was chosen Education Student of the Year, and a representative of Gamma Phi Beta sorority called the university to arrange a speaker for the next big pow-wow on education. My assumed prominence in the field was noted and I was assigned to represent the university. On the appointed day I had dyed some upholstery for a customer. The witch's brew she asked me to use was an acid green solution that smelled terrible. While getting ready for my presentation I found that the green stain wouldn't come off my hands, so I decided to keep my hands behind me or in my pockets.

I was minoring in speech, however, and the use of gestures was natural to me. So right in the middle of a point I was making I threw both hands up in the air. The first few rows of the audience gasped in horror at my apparent affliction, and they looked ill for the rest of my talk.

Most of us Varsity cleaners could be recognized at school by the stains of our trade. A janitor's shoe soles rotted off at the instep from frequent wading in hot chemical strippers, and the right side of a janitor's pants always sagged from carrying twenty pounds of keys around. Our wallets often picked up residue from the putty chisel we carried in our back pocket for scraping up sticky messes, and our neckties often had water stains at the tip from when we bent down to check the toilets on inspection day.

Some days we would be on a paint job and have to leave at 12:30 P.M. to make a 1 P.M. class, change clothes in the car, and rush into the class. In sociology class the girl sitting next to me seemed to be giving me frequent glances. My personal charm aside, I couldn't understand the attraction. Finally one day she couldn't contain herself any longer and she approached me. "Excuse me, sir, what are all those different colored spots on your ear?" (the roller flecks and paint drops I hadn't noticed or washed off in my haste to make class). I whispered back, "I have leprosy!" My popularity with her dropped instantly and the space between our chairs increased.

Soap, water, and elbow grease (plus a few brains) would seem to be the main ingredients of cleaning, but we soon realized that a more scientific approach meant more profit and a better job of cleaning. The most common of all cleaning tools (after soap and water) was the cloth or "rag." We learned fast to appear professional in our talk as well as our actions. Calling what we cleaned with a "rag" was crude, and sounded as if we might be using some stinky old T-shirt on the wall. Likewise, calling paint thinner "thinner" would often cause customers to flinch at the thought that we might be thinning paint before applying it. To enhance our image and build confidence, we would refer to our cleaning cloths as "towels," and to thinner as petroleum distillate or "enamel reducer." This vocabulary would bring smiles from the homeowners.

The towels were literally that—the thickest bath towels we could find cleaned much better than pieces of old sheet or bedspread. Our first towel supply came from the Varsity men scrounging up all of the spare towels around their homes. When that source was depleted, friends, neighbors, and relatives were tapped, and when that source gave out, we had to resort to buying towels. This was hard on the wives. We were all struggling to get through school, making do with repaired, patched, and used things and other get-by procedures, yet we'd go down to Penney's and buy the biggest, thickest, lushest, most deluxe bath towels, and then come home and cut them in half, fold them once, and sew them into an 11" x 14" tube that could be turned inside out when the outside got dirty. "Oh, let us use those towels just once before you cut them up to clean grease or wipe down toilets!" our wives would say. But seldom did this occur. The towels were bought and 90% of them were cut and sewed by Barbara, then they quickly went into service washing walls or in other cleaning.

When the towels were dirt saturated, we'd take them home or to the laundromat, wash them, dry them until they were nice and clean and fluffy again, and then start over.

Few laundromats (or for that matter wives) appreciated grungy towels swishing back and forth in their nice laundry facilities, but laundromats were open to the public after all. We were finally blackballed, however, after a catastrophe. We had used our towels to wipe up five gallons of spilled lacquer thinner on a job, then took the towels down and quickly washed them, not adding any soap because the towels usually contained soap from cleaning operations. Thus little of the volatile thinner was washed away. After washing, we threw the towels in a large gas dryer. Five minutes later there was a tremendous explosion, starring the dryer containing our towels. The lacquer fumes ignited and blew up the dryer and its surroundings, and we, our towels, and our reputation were thrown out—permanently.

Solvents always mean safety measures!

College-boy cleaners turned loose in a nice home with a picky owner often created "a situation." One home where Ralph Fry, a super polite and cultured Varsity veteran was running the job, the owner of the home, an elderly woman, was right behind the crew through just about every square inch of cleaning, checking their work with a magnifying glass. One of the crew returned to our shop to get some more towels and when he came back through the door the owner was nowhere to be seen (she was now sitting in a high-backed overstuffed chair that was facing the other way). The young man blurted out, "Is that old bag finally gone?" We all froze in embarrassment. Ralph very calmly, gesturing to the woman he was facing, said, "No, Mr. Brower, the lady of the house dwells at home." The "old bag" didn't even flinch, and eagled-eyed the job to the end.

Speak no evil of customers and clients, especially on the job. You might be surprised who's listening

A janitor's bad dream

"Special care" items usually call for special care every step of the way. Learn all you can about something in this category before you start in on it.

One of the worst things I ever experienced as a maintenance man occurred during a housepainting job for Mrs. Willis. We had worked for this woman before—she was a good customer and had boundless confidence in us. She wanted three rooms of her house painted this time and Arlo and I and two other of our best men took on the job.

When we arrived, we found that almost everything in the house had been moved out to the garage. The three rooms were bare except for three things: an enormous china closet, a huge mirror, and a small pet monkey in a cage (yes, a real, live, shrieking monkey!). The china closet (a 3-legged antique at least 7 feet high) was so heavy, she explained, that she just wanted us to move it away from the wall and paint around it. It was full of valuable antiques, she said, including some that were centuries old. There was precious dishware, stunning goblets and pitchers, plates with coats of arms and gold trim, silver salt and pepper shakers, etc.—a spectacular collection.

Arlo and I carefully took down the big mirror and moved it to the garage, mixed the paint, and the job began. We were painting the living room and soon reached the wall that the china cabinet blocked, so we prepared to move this tall treasure. It was heavy so we moved it very slowly about five feet away from the wall, and then went back to work. A minute later I heard a squeaking, creaking noise and glanced over my shoulder to see the large, heavy door of the cabinet swing slowly open. We learned later that years before, the front leg of the cabinet had been broken and after it was repaired the front leg was a little shorter than the other two. So when the door swung open, the unit was top heavy and it pitched forward and literally poured everything out onto the hardwood floor. By the time Arlo and I got to the closet it was empty and almost everything formerly in it was broken, even some of the silver things. It took four big boxes to gather up all of the remains of the once valuable collection.

Then I had to call Mrs. Willis. She was at her daughter's house next door, and was soon in deep despair over what happened, blaming herself for not telling us about the bad leg on this heirloom. We carried liability insurance, but as she said, there was no way insurance could replace the shattered heirlooms. It was a day of gloom and we did several hundred dol-

lars worth of extra work to try and compensate for what we couldn't help but feel was at least partly our fault.

At ten that evening, the paint was dry and we moved everything back into the house. When we went to the garage to get the precious mirror off the couch on which we had so carefully placed it, it had slipped down (with the help of some little neighbor boys playing cowboy in there) against some nearby chair legs. I was afraid to turn the mirror over, and when I did my fears were justified—it was broken.

That was more than I could take. This, too, wasn't our fault, but like the closet we were there and handled it, and should have kept an eye on it. I went out to a phone booth and called the owner of the glass store in town. "Hi, John—have you got an 84" by 48" prism edge mirror?" "I do have one exactly that size, an expensive lifetime Fuller mirror." "I want it!" "I'm sorry, Don, but I ordered that for Mrs. Van Snoot and she's waited two months for it. No way I can give it to you." Taking a big breath, I said, "Tell Mrs. Van Snoot two janitors' lives are at stake—it's a moral emergency!" He still refused, until I finally threatened to not buy any more paint from him. I met him at the store after hours and got the mirror and he ordered another for lady Van Snoot. The new mirror was exactly the same size as the old one and so we thought that after the day's turmoil we wouldn't say anything right now, just hang it up.

"Oh my," Mrs. Willis said smiling, "that is the most beautiful I've ever seen my mirror look—how did you do it?" So we confessed the second incident. "Oh, you didn't have to do that, boys—it wasn't your fault!" Mrs. Willis never filed an insurance claim and was a continuing customer, but to this day I haven't been able to blot from my memory the horrible sound of that beautiful collection breaking. We left that job with a lesson in graciousness unmatched—how could anyone be so kind after a visit from the three stooges plus an extra?

New employee surprises

When orienting new employees, don't take anything for granted. Some of the most obvious things might be the ones you forget.

In the mid sixties, when appearing on the media was really something, we got news that our newly hired secretary, Kathy, was one of the finalists for Miss Idaho and was going to be interviewed on the radio. Although she'd only been working for us for a couple of weeks, we were proud and the entire crew stopped work and assembled at the shop to listen. We had great expectations of a good plug of solid publicity for our enthusiastic little cleaning operation. There must have been a breakdown in our company training program, however. Here's how it went:

"Well, Kathy, it's good to have you on the show today. It must be exciting to be one of the finalists for Miss Idaho. Do you have a job?" asked the host.

"Yes."

"Who do you work for?"

"For Varsity Contractors."

"Great, and just what does Varsity Contractors do?"

"Uh, ah...I don't know what they do."

All of us listening moaned, and a few rolled on the floor. (She wasn't a blonde, either!)

Another time a bright-eyed, eager young woman joined our busy (and very informal), office as a secretary. It all had to be a little overwhelming, a consideration I always paid too little attention to—telling someone to "just do" things was more my style. When I couldn't remember a first or last name on the draft of a letter I would address the intended recipient "Dear Horsebreath," figuring that like my wife or the experienced secretaries she could find the real name in the file.

Two days later, quickly reviewing copies of recent letters, I found one perfectly typed and (gasp!) addressed to "Horsebreath Williams." Gulp, no... she wouldn't, she didn't... I ran to her desk, "You didn't mail this, did you?" "Oh yes, Mr. Aslett," she said in a innocent and obedient voice, "I typed it up carefully just like you wrote it." It was done, so why get upset. It ended up a cherished memory and a real bond between us, and no, Mr. Williams never said anything.

At a staggeringly busy time in my life when the amount of tax I had to pay made it seem like I was carrying the county single-handed, the local property tax assessor wanted an appointment to review my cleaning equipment at the shop so they could assess a healthy tax on this little company supporting a bunch of struggling college students, I asked him to wait a week or so until finals and a few pressing jobs were done. I intended then to give him a full and accurate list of all my machines, scaffolding, ladders, sprayers, buffers, buckets, etc. But he was rude and impatient, unconcerned with the taxpayer's convenience.

The day he decided to sneak into my shop was a day we had an emergency fire cleanup job underway and two extra crews working. We had just about everything I owned out on the job, even the wounded rug rakes. He slipped in and made his official list of what he saw, which wasn't much more than a couple of used desks. This made my tax for the year $6.92. I was so irritated by his invasion (the sneak!) that I never corrected his audit.

The image of our profession

There are no dead-end jobs, only dead-end attitudes.

My enthusiasm for our up-and-coming company blinded me at first to just where the janitor or cleanup person stood in our society's social strata. It didn't bother me then or now in the least if people couldn't tell the difference between the best profession in the world and all the others, but until it was less-than-subtly pointed out to me one day, I hadn't realized that being a janitor wasn't exactly something people were standing in line for.

An excerpt from my 1962 journal:

> Today had to be the epitome of how society views cleaning. I was working in the lobby of the First Security Bank's big, fancy office downtown, polishing the floor with a brand-new buffer (one I was really proud of). It was a high moment in my life—I was almost out of college, had a nice family, a great and growing little company, was a leader in school, church, and the community. I thought I was riding the tide of social prestige along with the rest of upstanding society. In the door came a late depositor, her deposit in one hand and a spoiled, whincy kid in the other. She dragged him through the doors past me, yanking his reluctant little arm, and finally shook him in disgust. "Behave, you little brat," she said in a stage whisper, and then pointing at me continued, "or you'll end up just like him!"

When we went places together my friends would introduce me as a businessman, and brag that I had many men working for me, fleets of trucks, etc. When the new acquaintances asked what kind of business, a silence would follow my answer and after a couple of desperate glances, they would swallow and say "a janitor??"

At class reunions or anywhere people were trying to impress each other with the longest, most official-sounding description they could come up with for their jobs, when I said "I'm a janitor" it was always good for a few gasps.

I worked to keep the men's enthusiasm for the business high, battling the janitor image. Occasionally a wife or two would make her husband aware of the fact that it was bad enough to be a toilet cleaner, but to advertise it to others wasn't too couth. Arlo's wife, Jackie, struggled with the image, as her husband, a pharmacy major, had worked his way through years of demanding pharmacy courses while humming "rub-a-dub-dub."

His real adjustment came, however, while he was working as a degreed pharmacist and still cleaning on the side.

We had a one-hour job to do at a freight terminal office, and since it was just a small job (and a day when few people would be there), Arlo and I didn't bother to put on uniforms or shave, and all of our good equipment was out on other jobs. We rummaged through some old supplies and managed to come up with the scroungiest mop imaginable, a couple of stiff paint-brushes, etc., and loaded them into the oldest truck we had. We were usually a classy operation, with polished trucks and clean uniforms, but we two bosses that morning looked as if the Salvation Army had outfitted us.

We reported to the job to dust some equipment, paint the floor, and sand some sheetrock. Paint-speckled, dirty, dusty, and dragging that wretched mop, we cut through the main terminal's plush lobby after we finished the job, and ran into one of the customers from the elite pharmacy Arlo worked at in his "day job." This particularly sharp, impeccably dressed woman thought of Arlo as the most dignified pharmacist in town. He filled all of her prescriptions and even mixed her super-secret underarm deodorant salve. She screeched to a halt, not believing her eyes. "Arlo, is that YOU?!!" Like the bottom hog at the trough he gulped and said weakly, "Hi, Mrs. Burnett."

"What are you doing?" she gasped.

"Well," he cleared his throat, "I have this little business on the side."

"But Arlo, a *janitor*??"

She then looked at me critically, wheeled, and retreated. Arlo mumbled some on the way home, "I looked like a troll, she was our best customer... wonder if she'll ever come in again." But from the next day on, Arlo was a true janitor, unfazed by any value judgment of his profession, ever after. (And before long he had joined the ranks of we full-time cleaners.)

We worked hard and disciplined fairly to maintain a clean reputation in a "dirty" business; as often back in the early days the people applying to work for a cleaning firm were those rejected from several other jobs. We did our best to find hard-working people of good character.

In spite of the often very limited options, we did manage to maintain a dignity admired by our colleagues. One approach I never forgot was when an applicant said to me during an interview, "Mr. Aslett, you have too many saints in your company—it's getting to be too goody-goody. You need to hire a good sinner or two like me." I'll admit that was a clever approach that caught me without a reply. I hired him, but never did notice any creative sinning afterward.

You're in the Army now!

Diplomacy is the word of the day, when introducing new tricks to old dogs... or anyone.

When I was nineteen, still a freshman at Idaho State, I heard that joining the National Guard was a good way to make some extra cash and maybe have a little immunity from being yanked out of school right now. So I joined "the Army" and I loved it! I'm not the kind of person who wants someone else to tell me when to breathe, eat, and change my underwear, but the order and discipline, the adventure and classes were wonderful. Learning marching and rifle team precision, driving a big tank and shooting a four-foot 75mm gun was sure fun for a farm boy.

Even my military training seemed to target my destiny, my hidden talents and skills. When orders were cut on bivouacs or barracks, I received latrine cleaning assignments often. Why this happened to such a good soldier as me no one knew. Although I never became a decorated hero on the battlefield, I was the undisputed colonel of the urinal!

I think the officers were a little shocked at my attitude of volunteering for everything—for the tear gas demonstration, guard duty in the motor pool, and yes, even doing the dishes in the mess hall, a massive cleaning experience in the camp barracks building.

The first day they put us back in the kitchen, where greasy dishes were sliding in from all sides, we had some Army (probably 1880) issue kitchen soap that just groomed the grease a little. No matter how much of it we used, or how long we soaked or scrubbed, it scarcely affected the slimy silverware or the stainless steel trays. It took six of us hours to get the dishes done. I took that for two meals, breakfast and dinner, then I walked down to the PX store, where you could buy normal dish detergent, and bought a jug of it. It was a good strong cleaner that could put grease on the run with one squirt. When those grease-coated cups and plates and trays came pouring in after supper, they hit that hot detergent solution and came out totally clean in a few seconds. In just thirty minutes we had all the dishes not just done but spotless, sparkling.

Word of "Aslett's kitchen platoon" leaked out via a brag by the supervisor of the mess hall, and soon the colonel came in to investigate. He looked at the dishes and the clock and he was amazed. How had we managed to outflank the forks and all? I snatched up the bottle of detergent, showed it to him, and said, "Here, Sir, we changed soap—that Army stuff is crap." Calling Army stuff crap (even if it is crap) is not a good approach to a colonel. Appalled, he snatched the bottle from me and commanded us to use Army standard issue. So we were reduced back to bathing the dishes in that worthless stuff and watching the grease float on top of the water instead of dissolve.

A couple of years later I was enrolled in Army ROTC at college. My shoes would get paint on them whenever I was painting with a roller, so a day or so before each Thursday's drill in ROTC, I would give them a coat of gloss black enamel paint. When the last drill of the year came around, the shoes were pretty heavy from those 36 coats of paint. They looked like something Ronald McDonald would wear. This particular drill was the grand finale of the year. A real Army general would be there for the occasion. All of our training would be displayed in this final inspection and drill out on the quadrangle area of the campus.

All week I reminded myself to give those rainbow brogans their last coating of black enamel, but not until after I had dressed and hustled to the quad did I glance down at my feet. With a horrible sick feeling, I realized I had forgotten to paint-shine my shoes. The company captain and two lieutenants had a conference as to what they would do to get me out of sight. Roadblock guard and supply-room guard were considered, but abandoned because I would be alone and noticed for sure. They decided to leave me in the platoon (one of nine) because they knew the "old man" would inspect only two or three platoons at most. The odds were good that I would be missed.

The band struck up a marching tune and we performed a marching spectacular with a snappy "eyes right" to the

overweight dignitary. We then stood at rigid attention as the general began to strut up and down the lines of men, eyeing his troops. He passed one, two, three, four platoons, came to ours, stopped, made a left face, and there was no doubt—we were lost! I was in the third column and as the snap of the rifle bolts drew closer I was eyes and Adam's apple from the ROTC commander. The general finally faced me, and his eye went from my paint-sprayed ears down to my ammonia-whitened hands and then to my decorated footwear. Our officers were frozen in their tracks. The commander looked back up at me, down at my shoes again. "My God," he said, easing away with a backward glance. The company commander who followed behind him gave me an "I'll kill you later" look. All year he had spelled my name with two s's (Asslett) and at that moment, I lived up to it!

> *Actually doing things is much better than re-*
> *peatedly reminding yourself to do them.*

CHAPTER 2

Earning and Learning Our Way

Launched into learning

THEY CALL gaining knowledge and experience a learning curve, and in the development of a cleaning business it was more like a learning cliff! Much can be said for the adventure of amateurism—mainly, there are few dull moments, as most real education results from pioneering and experimenting.

Because there was no letup in the need to support our families and my obligation to the other young men I'd hired who were also working their way through school, we took on all or any jobs available and made up processes as necessary, as we pretended and prayed to be seasoned professionals. We worked even harder, longer hours now, and willingly grabbed any cleaning challenge from our customers, finding ways to cut costs while upping quality.

Some people were impressed by our work, and a few depressed, but in the course of all of these projects and events we steadily gained real expertise.

No one who worked alongside of us could ever say cleaning was a routine job!

Doom at the top

Think new ideas all the way through, and test before you take a flyer!

As I designed and planned for the expansion of my company, I was determined to cut costs and nonproductive time. One sudden stroke of brilliance here almost cost me my life.

It was near the end of my college days, and cedar shingle roofs were popular. But they needed to be maintained. This was usually done by applying a mixture of linseed oil and graphite. A bag of graphite dust was mixed with linseed oil and left to sit overnight. The next morning, after the dew was gone from the roof, a couple of us would climb up with buckets and brushes and dip into the mixture and work it into the roof. It didn't take long to apply the material, but getting the ladder, roof jacks, and other equipment in place on the roof was time consuming. We would generally hook an extension ladder over the peak of the roof to hang on to and use as a stairway as we applied the coating, and move the ladder as we worked our way across the roof.

We always wore tennis shoes for good traction, because graphite is one of the slickest substances known to man and combined with oil it made for treacherous treading. Once the mixture got on your shoes, the honeymoon was over and you began worrying about your life—the steeper the roof, the bigger the risk.

A new invention came out about this time called the "airless" spray gun. This could spray a strong stream of material over a three-foot span, and cover an unbelievable amount of area quickly. It was easy to see that if a way to maneuver around on a roof faster could be found, this spray gun could be a big boost to the profit column. For weeks I thought about it, conjuring up everything from helicopters to sixty-foot poles, but nothing seemed really practical until... sure, why not? Some spike-soled logging boots! If lumberjacks could leap around on bobbing logs in the water with them, I should be able to perform like Fred Astaire on a pitched wooden roof; finish one in an hour instead of the seven or eight it ordinarily took now.

When I rushed to town to pick up a pair, I discovered that not every store carried such things. In fact, none of them did. In

Montgomery Ward one day I asked the shoe salesman if by any chance he knew where I could secure a pair of logging boots. "Why, yes, Sir, I do, in fact I have a pair right here." He left and came back with a big box. "We never carry these but someone ordered them and then never came back." Out they came and they were beauts—fourteen inches high with a sole armed with neat rows of long, sharp spikes. (Even if they were size 11 and I wore an 8.) They generally sold for $150 but he would sell them to me for $60. I walked out of the store whistling, "Bring on the roof!"

My song was answered in less than a week when a large church in Downey, Idaho, asked us to graphite and oil their roof. Like an athlete dressing for the game of his career, I carefully (with four pair of socks) slipped on my prize boots. They gave me a feeling of power as I crunched across the lawn and started up the ladder. First one step on the roof, and then another, and another, and such a steep roof! I was ecstatic—my brilliant invention was working! I grabbed the airless gun, tromped across the shingles like a Swiss mountaineer, and began to spray, calculating that I'd have the whole $250 job done in two hours.

I was at the height of my glory for at least ten minutes with my trusty spikes gripped into the shingles, and the crew on the ground cheering. There was, however, a flaw in the engineering of the situation. The soles of the boots had to be parallel with

the roof for the spikes to make contact, so I had to bend at my ankles to the pitch of the roof—this was hard as the boots were high and stiff, and as my ankles weakened the spikes lost contact and the steel-hard leather of the sole edges made contact with the graphite instead. As gravity took over, the sides of the boots hitting and my fingernails trying to dig into the evenly spaced shingles made a nice clickety-clack in perfect rhythm, and stopped only when I sailed off the two-story roof. I would have died with my boots on, but providence was kind because the architect had provided a roofed entryway to the building and after a fall of only five feet, I landed on it unharmed.

I unlaced my marvelous discoveries and donated them to the next garage sale. A lucky lumberjack who wore size 11 walked away with them for $16 (probably the guy who ordered them in the first place).

Caught short!

Any material that can shrink usually will in the cleaning process. Be aware of what the things you are about to clean are made of—including the small parts.

At this point in time we were cleaning a lot of those big old venetian blinds, and one day we got a call from the county courthouse, the largest building in Pocatello—three stories high and a block long. What did they want? A dream come true—all of the blinds cleaned. There were more windows on that place than on a Chicago train, and I bid the job and got it. These were not small blinds—some were ten feet wide and over eight feet tall. We took them all down, keeping careful track of which window they came off of, took them to our shop, and cleaned them. They came out nice, and I sent a couple of the crew to hang them back up. It was Saturday and this took most of the day.

Sunday morning, on the way to church, I swung by the courthouse to admire our primo job and—gasp!—under each blind there was a foot of space. They were twelve inches short of the windowsill. "Oh, those dumb drama majors who hung them must have got the wrong blinds on the wrong windows," I decided, until I drove around the other side of the building and saw that all three floors of blinds were a foot short. Gadfrey—did we get the wrong blinds? After I scratched my head for a few minutes, I realized that the ribbons on commercial building blinds were cloth, not plastic like most of the home blinds we'd cleaned, and they must have shrunk! That was a long Sunday afternoon, night, and couple of days that followed as we had to take all of the blinds down, re-wet them, and rehang them with weights, just enough weight to pull them down to the sill. I'll never forget those hundreds of clothes hangers with whatever we could find to add weight dangling from them.

The great blinds cleaning machine

Test before you make a full-size model! Not even geniuses can ignore physics and logistics!

As noted earlier, I was always looking for a way to do a job faster, better, and cheaper. Since we were now cleaning blinds by hand, laying them out on a padded surface and scrubbing them with a soft brush, I figured if I could invent a machine to clean them, I'd be rich, famous, and home more. So I designed an oversized vat that looked like a giant paint roller pan which could be filled with soapy water, and then a big cylinder of screening (eight feet long and four feet in diameter) which rotated in the pan like one of those riverboat paddlewheels. I mounted a large electric motor on the outside of the vat and attached it by pulleys to the cylinder. It was one big project and after it came together I had it galvanized to prevent rust. It cost a lot and it weighed... well, you don't really want to know. But it was beautiful, and I got newspaper coverage as far away as Salt Lake City for inventing it. The only trouble was it didn't work.

When the long-awaited day of tryout finally came, we hauled a load of blinds from some office and I strapped one to the clever hooks on the cylinder and switched that baby on. Two things were shredded instantly—the blind and my dreams. The drum moved so fast that the blind was ripped to pieces in about fifteen seconds, so I didn't have to face the bigger question of how to heat up 300 gallons of water and keep it hot (I think I finally determined that it would cost $46 a blind to heat that massive pool to the right temperature). Then, too, I hadn't crimped the sheet metal of the vat and it buckled from the weight of all that water. There wasn't a part of the whole thing that worked well. All that time, expense, and anticipation and it crashed.

The owner of a local café did give me $20 to use the cylinder for a revolving sign until people complained about how ugly it was. And a farmer bought the tank for watering cattle. Both were local—I should have sold these things somewhere far away so I didn't have to see them daily! A laugh now, but a real low back then when I had to face up to all of this lost time and money.

Gloss finish high!

I painted and sealed surfaces for years after the following in properly ventilated settings, and never hiccupped again. Ventilate, and read the label!

Varsity men often got professional painter's licenses, and pro painters often warned us that painters sometimes ended up winos. I'd made it through thirty-five years without ever tasting any type of alcohol, so I didn't see much chance of ending up in the gutter by this route. Until I learned that there were other ways to get intoxicated.

We always thought we were happy at the end of an enamel paint job because the job was over. But not so—it was the paint fumes that elated our tired bodies. One day Arlo, who had never imbibed anything stronger than a Fresca, locked himself in a tiny bathroom with a gallon of high quality enamel. He had been careful to close every vent, window, and door to prevent airborne dust and debris from defiling his paint job. He went in irritable and anxious to be done and get back to his job at the pharmacy. He emerged two hours later somewhat less than coherent. His eyes were glistening, he stuttered and drooled as he spoke, and even laughed agreeably when we told him his wife had called and said their septic tank had overflowed. He was rummy.

Another time, we contracted to paint a large church building in a rural area and the ladies' auxiliary offered to feed us at the church to save us from trying to find local diners, which didn't exist then in the town of Teton, Idaho. Our ten-man crew had sprayed and rolled thirty gallons of enamel onto the halls and classrooms by noon. The ladies were delighted with our sparkling, happy manner as we wolfed down our food. They informed us that the supper meal was going to be even better (we would still be there, since we still had another fifty gallons to spray and roll onto the big auditorium/cultural hall and exterior of the building). They came through with another fine meal that evening and it was consumed by some rather silly young men. The women eyed us suspiciously now, our trustworthiness in question as they spied pantyhose tied around our necks and protruding from our back pockets. Unfortunately they didn't understand how paint fumes could affect behavior, or that pantyhose is unequalled for straining paint to keep the sprayer from plugging up. The resulting gossip and a similar job in Jackson Hole, Wyoming, led us to wearing masks and paying a little more attention to ventilation.

In Jackson, we spray-painted a big old cathedral being made over into a restaurant. We noticed many flies when we started work but never saw any more during the job. The next morning we walked into a marvelous surprise. There was no red carpet anywhere, but a deep carpet of dead flies. It was almost unbelievable, and walking across them made a crunching noise. The fumes must have killed them.

What goes up must come down

There are few things more seductive—and dangerous—than a temporary fix.

There were other dangers for the unaware in painting. My brother Larry and I had contracted to clean and paint the recreation hall ceiling of a large church in Rexburg, Idaho, and to reach that 25-foot height, planned to use a portable scaffolding base mounted on large rubber caster wheels. When we started a job we would simply stand four 4" x 4" pillars up on end, nail them on, and quickly construct the rest of the scaffolding with 2" x 4"s and plywood.

They were holding an evening meeting in the chapel of the church and Larry and I were on the other side of the curtain constructing the scaffolding. Until we were sure we had reached the right height, we only tacked each plank on with a nail or two and at some point decided to get up on the scaffold and see if we could reach the ceiling. Not thinking about our poor nailing job, both of us climbed up on the platform to the top and discovered the height was just right. To celebrate, I did a little jig, which caused our combined 350 pounds to be just too much for the nails, and the entire scaffold collapsed. I mean it disintegrated—those 20-foot 4" x 4"s all fell out and the platform and all of the cross-members went down. It happened so fast there was no time to jump away. The noise in the room was like a bomb going off when it all (plus Larry and I) came down. The people in the church meeting thought the spirits were coming and Larry and I thought our spirits were going, but neither happened. By some fortunate circumstance of the way we rode the platform down, neither of us was seriously hurt. We shortened the church meetings and lengthened the number of nails in the scaffolding after that.

All in a night's work

A little floor-buffing job at a local discount center seemed routine and simple, but it wasn't. Arlo arrived there one evening at 11 P.M. (after closing time), unlocked the front door, and felt his way into the back office where the switch for the lights was located. As he concentrated on finding the panel box, he thought he heard someone breathing close by. The hair on the back of his neck stood up as he scanned the darkness. Sure enough, someone was right next to him—a young burglar with a revolver in his hand! Arlo, who was armed only with a putty knife for scraping gum off the floor, hollered in a loud, gruff voice, "What are you doing in here?!"

The undoubtedly inexperienced burglar, overcome by the authority of Arlo's demand, dropped the gun in the wastebasket and ran out the door. Arlo ran after him, captured him, and called the police. Soon an officer was leading the shaking and unsuccessful thief to a squad car. But as the officer put him in the back seat of the car and walked around to the driver's door, the burglar jumped out and took off at a dead run. The officer was no match and was soon left behind. The burglar got away and the building received its usual sweeping and buffing. Arlo's work report read: "Normal evening. P.S. Caught a burglar."

Bullied by a buffer

Before you restart a machine, think: "What was it doing when the power went off?"
Don't do anything from "around the corner."

Only a few weeks after this, about midnight, I was cleaning part of a telephone building myself to make sure nothing went wrong because of a recent slip and fall incident that had happened there. I was using a huge 120-pound floor machine to buff the floor in the women's locker and lounge area. A buffer of this size has unbelievable torque and can be hard to control, but if you know what you are doing it can be operated with two fingers. There is a big drive block under the machine faced with an inch-thick rubber pad that holds the nylon pad that buffs the floor. To make things easier I had the automatic switch on (a sort of "cruise control") that would keep the buffer going without having to constantly squeeze the trigger. I was right in the middle of the ladies' lounge when the cord unplugged and the buffer stopped. I skipped to the end of the cord, brought it to a closer outlet, and plugged it in. But I made one little mistake. The automatic switch was still engaged and as fate would have it, one of the oldest of the hundred operators who worked there came stiffly hobbling by. I was around the corner when I plugged it back in, and that woman was only three feet from the buffer when it engaged.

Without someone to control it, the big machine started with a leap. Right at the woman it came, and knocked her down. The nylon pad came out from under the machine, leaving nineteen inches of rubber grabbing at the linoleum. This gave the buffer incredible traction. As the woman scrambled to her feet and started to run, screaming, the machine kept moving in her direction. Two more big leaps and it caught up with her and beat her to the floor again. I was around the corner by now and saw what had happened. Her shoe was literally ripped from her foot and torn almost in half. She lay cringing in the corner by the time the machine finally pulled its plug out again.

I wasn't even going to bother finishing the job—I knew Varsity had had it! The woman (a supervisor) got up, looked at me and the buffer, and said, "My word!" and with her broken shoe in hand hobbled to the lounge to recover. The most unbelievable part of the incident is that she never said one word to anyone about it, nothing! Per procedure, the chief operator of the phone building had a big tally book and anything unusual or out of line was usually carefully reported. This never was. Perhaps the woman thought if she talked we'd send the buffer after her again. Anyway, my salute to her. What a woman—she wouldn't even let us replace the shoe!

Courtesy of Mr. Clean

Religion is best kept out of polite dinner parties, and our on-the-job activities. The workplace isn't a congregation conveniently assembled for us to address.

Another time, I contracted to paint the walls and some product stands at a local supermarket, which proved to be a very creative experience. They wanted two coats of paint sprayed on twenty-five island-type stands and a magazine rack. I was locked in the store per security policy to do the job, and I assured them I would be through before the next morning at 8 A.M. when they returned to let me out.

I started in with my compressor at 10 P.M. and by 3 A.M. it was done. Since this was fast-drying paint, and I had four hours more of "confinement," I decided I'd be a good fellow and put all of the magazines back in the rack for them. Being a literature student at the university, I was critical of garbage publications such as supermarket "rag mags," pornography, and the like, and disliked seeing them displayed in public. The paint fumes must have gotten to me because I decided to set the magazine rack up in a very moralistic and subjective manner. I placed the girlie, movie star, and other "unfit" material behind *Better Homes, Sunset, Reader's Digest, Popular Mechanics*, and the *Saturday Evening Post*. When I finished, there was the huge magazine rack with its fresh coat of paint, now rated "G." It was magnificent—not a questionable publication showing anywhere. I left the store feeling I'd contributed greatly to the edification of society. A raving phone call from the store manager two hours later indicated that he did not share my value system. The language that he used would have diluted greatly the "G" rating of the display. Thus a nonroutine paint job ended.

Mile high cleaning

Cleaning can be a high both literally and figuratively!

In the cleaning business, most jobs were full of adventure, education, and new friends and acquaintances. Some of these were truly hard work but we couldn't wait to tackle them.

In the late seventies we signed a rather unique contract with the Utah Parks Service, the agency that operated three big national parks in Southern Utah: Bryce Canyon, Zion National Park, and the North Rim of the Grand Canyon.

These contain some of the most magnificent rock formations in the world, and sunrises and sunsets there awe onlookers. All of these natural attractions had such heavy snows that they were only open for the summer season. As soon as the weather allowed entrance, a few weeks before the parks opened, our well organized and experienced cleaning and maintenance team would arrive with truckloads of equipment and open up the lodges, shops, cabins, restaurants, dining rooms, and other rooms and clean them. We dusted the towering forty-foot rafters, rock walls, fireplaces, and everything else inside, stripped and waxed floors, shampooed carpets, sanitized restrooms, washed walls, sanded and revarnished hardwood floors, and cleaned windows and counters and display cases, removing the cobwebs of winter and all the traces of last summer's tourist wear and tear. We also raked the grounds and paths and cleaned them of debris.

We did this before the concessionaires and park staff arrived. We stayed in the cabins in the park while we were there, and the park department sent a cook who fed us like kings!

The work was hard fourteen-hour days, but it was pure heaven. We had the parks to ourselves—there was no one but us amidst those massive wonders of nature. It was quiet beyond quiet, and birds, deer, and squirrels were all over, unafraid. There was no litter, no cars, no phones, no commerce—the peace and majesty of it all was unmatched.

The North Rim of the Grand Canyon was the last to be finished, because of the deep snow. That was a beautiful place to finish a long, tough job. Bryce Canyon was breathtaking, but I loved the Grand Canyon. The ghost of greatness lingered in the old buildings, and there was real power in the canyon's massive size and depth. Soon everything was gleaming for opening day. It was a great experience and Varsity can claim a record matched by no other window cleaners in the world: we cleaned the exterior lodge windows overlooking one of the most dramatic parts of the canyon, and one mile from the ground is high window washing! Mark Browning, a fearless mountain climber, hung on a rope outside the lodge to do it. No skyscraper wimp in a big city has even come close to that record. We used to have a waiting list to get chosen for that job.

I was so anxious one spring to get on the job at the North Rim that I went by the calendar instead of calling ahead to see if it had opened. We arrived at the pre-entry gate twenty miles from the complex after a 450-mile drive from Pocatello, only to find the gate closed and locked. We could see ten-foot snowdrifts across the road. There were no cell phones in the sixties, so we sat in the double-cab International pickup for hours pondering what to do when a large snowplow (with a key) finally showed up and plowed the road into the park as we followed. I think this was in May!

When we reached that secluded "resort city" closed for the past five months, the bearded artist who volunteered as a watchman came blinking out to meet us, happy to see another human. Everything was shut down and boarded up, water and electricity turned off, and worst of all, no cook, no food. It was two days before the rangers and mechanics would show up, and the only thing we had to eat was the remains of a frozen sack of last year's garden carrots left in the back of our pickup. In this case, the crew was not convinced this was a fun adventure!

The baptism of a bad bid

Some of the magic words (buzzwords, if you will) of the cleaning business—or any business—can help out in those tricky situations. Learn all you can, and have them handy.

Whenever I bid a job, I wanted to get it so I pursued every angle possible to get the job done well and fast, and make a profit in the end. No matter how good you get at this, however, you still miss a few by under or overbidding. When you realize you have miscalculated or left something important out of the initial quote, you take it on the chin; unless there is some better and faster way to do a good job than the way you originally planned.

Cleaning the main lodge at the North Rim of the Grand Canyon one year, I bid to vacuum the dust, dead bugs, and cobwebs off the twenty foot high, sixty foot long rock wall at the end of the main dining hall, figuring one of us could get up on a tall ladder with a backpack vacuum strapped to our back and in five or six hours cover the whole wall. When we arrived to do the job, I realized it was going to be much more difficult than I'd imagined to reach in and get decades' worth of dirt and debris out (there was still mortar dust there from its construction in 1924) and we didn't have a ladder or scaffolding capable of reaching the top. I feared it would actually take about two days to do the quality job I had bid. Then my eye fell on a heavy-duty hose—not just a wimpy garden hose but a real professional model more than an inch in diameter, with water pressure to spare.

My crew and I were the only ones there, since the park hadn't yet opened for the year, and surely, I rationalized, hosing down the wall would do a much better job than vacuuming it. I had fishing boots in the truck, so I put them on and we moved all of the tables and chairs out of the dining room to the sun room. Then I reeled out the hose and turned the water on full bore.

Man, when that water, strong as the stream from a fire hose, hit that wall, dirt, dust, grit, and the carcass of every form of bug life in the canyon was flushed out, and came cascading down the wall. Bonanza! The wall looked like new! As soon as the water hit the tile floor, I had two guys with floor squeegees push the runoff across the floor, through the big double doors, over the cliff, and down into the canyon.

When we were about three-quarters through, it looked as if every plumbing pipe in the complex had broken. I looked up and there stood the head of Utah Parks, and his boss. He and his fellow manager were stunned at the scene. I was terrified, but I waded over to them enthusiastically in my hip boots through three inches of water and shouted, "Can you believe how good that wall looks, Lamar? Looks better than new, doesn't it?" He gave a feeble affirmative nod. "Vacuuming just didn't do the job, so we are biting the bullet and giving you a deluxe, expensive wash job for the same price." ("For the same price" always

pleases people, even if they don't know what the original price was.) "We are getting the floor clean, too, in the process. Just look at the grime coming out of those rocks—we are doing a cleaning job that's been overdue for forty years."

By now the two of them were nodding admiringly at the results and the savings, and walked on, satisfied, through the complex. And it did look super, three times as good as vacuuming would have done, and in only one hour—we made a nice profit in the end. I'm just glad the floor was the old linoleum and not wood or carpet! They even hired us again the next year!

Going for the gold

Competing for excellence can make work fun!

All of the managers in our company were paid by the job, not the hour, so speed and efficiency really mattered. We always ended up making a game of work, and would race to see who of us could clean, paint, wax, or buff the best and fastest. We always went for "janitor records"—doing things faster, better, higher, etc.

You might see four of us on a twenty-four foot painter's plank set up beneath four fifteen-foot high church windows (full of little 8" x 10" panes), all of us with small brushes in one hand and a gallon pail of white paint in the other. We'd be trimming the window sashes, cutting a perfect knife-clean edge between paint and glass—no masking tape or rags allowed! We were all expert painters and all thought we were the best and would each take one of those giant windows and race top to bottom. It was so close one or two bad strokes and you lost. We were concentrating so intensely breathing almost got in the way. After an hour the finish was usually so close we were within one or two panes of each other, just minutes apart. Mark Browning, often the winner, was ambidextrous (as proficient with his left hand as his right). So he just changed arms when the rest of us had to shift position. It was a blast!

Cleaning up and setting things up was so much fun we forgot it was work. New employees thought we were crazy at first, but caught on quick.

Cleaning on and off the wall

Most of the Varsity people were full of enthusiasm and color—they had to be to survive the constant pressures of our calling. Since we were working daily in people's homes and offices, I also needed people of strong character.

I was hiring mostly college students but occasionally found a good high school senior. One individual I hired this way was Duane Hansen, who looked like a big draft horse. He worked for me through his senior year of high school and another year, then left for two years on a church mission. When he came back at age twenty-one he was husky, handsome, and clean cut, on to college now and ready to meet the world. He was to experience some unique adventures for a returned missionary.

We received a smoke loss job in a downstairs restaurant; and while we cleaned it the proprietor of the small hotel upstairs was impressed and asked us to clean some of her halls and rooms. I wasn't aware of all of the activities that were available in that popular off-road hotel, and my innocent, unmarried employee Duane was scheduled for the day. He had no sooner set up his ladder in the hall to scrub the walls when a vivacious little red-head, clad in considerably less than street clothing, waltzed out of one of the rooms to pick up a customer. She stopped and

admired Duane's skill and questioned him about how the wall machine worked, and then slithered on down the hall. All day the girls, especially the redhead, came by this handsome hunk of man laboring away, popping peanuts in his mouth, and counseling him never to get involved with girls of their profession. Duane finished the job with sweat on his forehead and steam coming out of both ears!

A sticky situation

Give it the eye before you apply, and don't take success for granted.

The huge student union building at Idaho State University was the center for breaks, social events, bowling, pool, and eats. Though my tuition fees had helped pay for its construction, even when I was a student at the university, my activities there had been confined to selling the products used to maintain the building to the custodial staff. At first I sold mops, then scrubbing pads and wax. Eventually I was selling almost every product used to clean the student union, except one; terrazzo sealer for the seeming acres of terrazzo floors in the building.

I was making a respectable profit from my sales, and it appeared the account would last forever. Still I wasn't satisfied—greed can crumble great attainments. I kept pushing the terrazzo seal and when I promised that I would apply it myself to the entire first floor of the building, they finally agreed to buy and try it. We picked a quiet Wednesday evening and after the last student had retreated to the dormitories, moved in the floor equipment. We scrubbed the terrazzo, leaving the surface ready for a fresh coat of my seal. After I applied it, it looked as if a brilliant sheet of glass had been laid over the floors. It was 5:30 in the morning when I loaded my equipment back in the truck and went home. I knew the student union director would be pleased with the job and call to compliment me on the improvement.

At 7:20 A.M., the phone rang and it was the director. He was excited, all right, but not in the way I had in mind. "Aslett, there are going to be 5,000 students down here today and this floor is wet and sticky," he yelled.

"It couldn't be," I comforted him, "that seal dries in thirty minutes." He groaned and moaned and threatened me, informing me that I'd better have the problem corrected within the next fifteen minutes. I leaped out of bed, rushed to the student union building, and examined the floor finish I'd applied. My heart sank—the seal, which normally dried in forty-five minutes or less, for some reason hadn't set up and was the consistency of syrup. I had single-handedly closed the student union building; my popularity with the director dissolved, and I lost the whole account in one day.

Years later, as I gained more knowledge of chemicals and flooring, I understood why it hadn't dried. The waxy polish normally used on it had penetrated the pores of the terrazzo and although it appeared clean after we washed it, it wasn't, and the oily residue on it retarded the drying time.

Signing on... and off

Consider reality as well as romance when branching out in your business.

I always had a secret love for art and advertising, and even took a correspondence course from an art instruction school when I was twenty-nine. My brother Larry, who had worked for me in college and was now in construction work, was a good artist and painter, so I asked him to join me in starting a little sign company. Lettering buildings and vehicles and making custom signs always seemed fascinating to me—creating things everyone looked at and that often altered life in some way.

We called the business Totem Signs, and quickly found out that our view of this business was more romanticism than reality. There weren't as many signs needing to be made as we had imagined, and there were more good, experienced sign companies out there than we had been aware of. Roadside billboards had a meager, long-term (like twenty years from now) return. We did do a couple of high-altitude signs, including one on the front of an airport hangar, where we deserved to die on the jury-rig scaffolding we arranged atop those 1890s decaying brick parapets. People liked Larry's work but paid little and late, so we did other painting work to supplement the sign income.

My big debut (and only moment of glory) came when I suggested to the small grocer of our little hometown of McCammon that he should cover the south side of the store's cinderblock wall with an attractive sign which I would do in exchange for $43 worth of groceries (you see why we were never profitable). He said okay and I drew up a tempting thumbnail sketch of a sack of groceries, with celery and all kinds of things sticking out of the top, and a large "Howell's Market" lettered on the other side. I was a good letterer. But the sack of groceries ended up a waste of good paint. Looking at art on billboards is sure easier than producing it. My celery looked like sagebrush, my can of beans like a mini leaning tower of Pisa, the loaf of bread looked like a bald head with wrinkles, and the bag itself looked thoroughly recycled. I took the $43 worth of groceries but never parked on that end of the lot again. Fortunately, someone ran into the wall and knocked a big hole in my infamous painted bag and when the wall was fixed it was painted over. After that, I was demoted to the office end of the operation.

Other, more interesting and profitable businesses came along and this business, like most of our signs, gradually faded away (although a few, after 35 years, were still up!), and the company was blended into Varsity.

A convicted criminal:
The State of Idaho vs. Don A. Aslett

High jinks can have a high cost.

Keith Hall and David Johnson were both fine young men, and full of energy and fun. Through the summer of 1965 (after I had graduated from college and was teaching school while running my cleaning business on the side) we laughed, played, and worked hard together, and a great friendship developed between us. Both boys were leaders in school and the community. The two of them had driven to a small farm town with me on Labor Day to finish a job prior to the start of school. Heading home, we passed a lot where the state highway department had left several pieces of heavy equipment parked. As we drove by, David quipped, "Boy, Mr. Aslett, that's just what you need to level the road on your new ranch!" (He was referring to a big yellow road grader sitting on the lot). "It sure is," Keith joined in. I answered that there was no chance in the world of hiring a state road grader for a private road, and forgot about the whole thing.

Four hours later, as I was working in the yard, I spotted a big yellow grader coming across the valley. I knew it couldn't be, but... my intuition told me it could be. When the grader slowed up at my gate and turned in, I knew it was! I ran to the gate waving my arms in alarm and sure enough, there sat the two faithful Varsity men, in their white uniforms with a big Varsity emblem on the front. "Are you guys crazy?" I yelled. "Get that thing out of here!" "Oh, don't worry, Mr. Aslett, it's in good hands," and they lowered the blade with great glee and began to grade my lane (the one leading from the road to my house). They were both good mechanics, and I learned later that they had fixed a flat tire on the machine, hot wired it to start it, and drove it three miles over the interstate to my house. I pleaded with the two students to return the dirt-moving demon and they, high on their high jinks, assured me that they would take all responsibility for it.

After a few passes up and down my road (which they left in far worse shape than it had been), they pulled around the front of the house to make a pass over the front yard. There was a big hole there and they hit it. The front wheel dropped into the pit up to the axle, but unaware of this, they shifted the machine into reverse and backed up. A road grader has tremendous power and traction. The front wheel shifted sideways, the steering bolt snapped, and the two front wheels collapsed. There sat the grader on the highest knoll in the area, unmovable.

It was a holiday so no heavy equipment places were open. Needless to say the two boys panicked, realizing there was now no way to return the "borrowed" piece of road equipment. A neighbor who saw the grader perched on the hill (and hated to miss out on any kind of action) drove down to see if he could help. He provided a large railroad bolt that was lying around his place and in a few hours the wheels were restored to a less than perfect alignment. Keith and David couldn't get the grader out of the yard quick enough now, and soon it was limping down the road, with the two front wheels tilting awkwardly inward and leaving a trail of black rubber from my gate back to the state parking lot.

Two days later, while I was working on our new house with my mother-in-law there, the glass man installing glass, and two or three friends visiting, up the lane came the county sheriff. He got out of his car and shuffled over to the front yard, on which there was a large set of cleat tracks, and pieces of broken yellow parts scattered here and there. "Don, the State of Idaho has reported a road grader stolen and damaged. I heard reports it was out here." I told him the story and he said, "Well, no problem. I'll visit the boys." He talked to the boys, who were then charged with stealing the grader and were to appear in court. I was to attend also, not on charges but to plead for leniency. When the day came, there sat their mothers, weeping; their innocent boys (neither of whom had ever been in trouble before in their lives) standing before the judge. They were sentenced to make a donation to a boys' ranch and some other things in lieu of a heavy fine as the judge had a sense of humor and didn't consider this a malicious premeditated act.

I drove back to my teaching job, relieved that it was all over. Little did I know that my road grader problems had just begun. Two weeks later, I received a call on the intercom during 4th period English class. "Don," a voice on the other end said, "This is Jack [the sheriff]. I've just been handed a warrant for your arrest from the State of Idaho. Shall I come down and get you or do you want to stop by?" Not anxious to expose my students to any hint of criminal activities, I agreed to meet him and we went to the local judge, who read me the charges. "Don Aslett did go onto said property and remove said machine on said day, in violation of Idaho State code 125-00045982." I pleaded not guilty in any sense and the judge said a hearing would be set up and I would be contacted.

I walked out again relieved. The two district judges knew me as an honest, industrious teacher and toilet cleaner and surely if I just explained the circumstances, I would be vindicated. I decided it was silly to even think of getting an attorney. It would just take Keith and David with me, and a few words from them would clear everything up. My neighbor Ernie was the manager of a savings and loan company and warned me to get an attorney, saying that anyone who represents himself has a horse's rump for a client.

I received notice that the hearing would be in my hometown of McCammon at the local judge's house, not in the Pocatello district court as I had assumed. I felt a little impulse at last to call an attorney, but dismissed the thought. The two boys and I showed up at 2 P.M. The hearing was held in the living room of the judge's small, cluttered home. A soap opera was blaring away on the TV, the judge was unshaven, and his boots were untied. There were a few others there; a couple of relaxed kids, a lounging dog, a state policeman (there on other business), a local deputy, and a representative from the State of Idaho. The state man stood and read the charges and listed the cost of the damage. The name Aslett was well known in the construction and road building business. My grandfather had fifteen children, thirteen of them boys, all of whom became associated with Grandpa Aslett in the construction field. An Aslett could run any heavy equipment made—except for me, that is. I was a farmer, teacher, and janitor. I stood and explained my side of the story carefully and ended with, "So you see, your Honor, I had nothing at all to do with it, and the boys have been tried, convicted, and punished for the crime." While I was talking and pleading, I was standing by the judge's desk, and I watched him write out:

Damages $270

Fine $500

30 days in jail

Etc.

When I sat down, the judge, without hearing from the boys or any further discussion, creaked to his feet and said, "Huh, it's easy to see that you put them up to it, and likewise you are an accessory. How could they know how to run the thing?" Being a former debate student, I tied him in a knot in a minute with questions like, "You mean to tell me Sears is guilty of that murder in Pocatello last week because they sold the gun used? If it hadn't been for Sears the guy wouldn't have shot the other guy?"

This proved to be a mistake and enraged the old gentleman. He leaped to his feet and said, "I find you guilty as charged, fine you, sentence you," etc. I couldn't believe what I was hearing. "This is a hearing and under Idaho law a hearing can't be used to determine final guilt," I said. He roared back, "I have the jurisdiction to change this hearing to a trial and I hereby do so!" (Something like that.)

One of the boys jumped up to the rescue and was told by the judge to shut up and sit down. I refused to pay and told the judge he was a ridiculous spectacle. The deputy there prepared to haul me off to jail. The state policeman was much more versed on the law than the others, and informed them that they couldn't jail me, that I could post bail. This quieted everyone down. I posted a big bail and was a free man for the day.

I left the house convicted of a felony and sentenced in the official records of the court. One of the best criminal attorneys in the area, Herman McDevitt, had often been a guest lecturer and evaluator for my college debate team. His sister was my partner for a few debates and I'd known Herman for years, so I called him. He shook his head in disbelief and said sarcastically, "Don, with your reputation around here, if you'd committed a nice clean rape or murder I could get you off, but this... we have a hassle coming." (Ironically Herman was then on a committee to stamp out the injustices of the small-town judges.)

Meanwhile Ernie, the helpful neighbor, decided to try and restore the damage done to my image in the community. He called Keith and David (still the two most popular seniors in school) and convinced them that they had inflicted a great injustice on Mr. Aslett and the right thing to do was to go to church next Sunday and stand up in front of the congregation and confess their crime to exonerate me. Big mistake. They both did it, in tears, and every person in there pilloried the boys and glared daggers at me—I lost what little image I had left, for sure.

The case continued for a few months until the judge died of a heart attack and not long afterward I received a letter dismissing all charges. Keith and David paid the lawyer's fees out of their next summer's wages and it was over at last.

The excess express

Clutter makes every job take longer.

Just about the time you figured you'd seen about everything on a cleaning job, something new would surface. One morning we got a call from Yellowstone Insurance Adjusters. They had a fire loss job in a three-bedroom home, so we went to bid on it. A fire in the basement had burned the floor joists badly—the rest of the house was okay, but heavily smoked. There was sticky smoke residue on and in everything.

The owners were real collectors, and had more stuff than anyone I'd ever seen. The job took us a month and from our final count, after cleaning (and billing), I remember two things. In the ordinary house fire damage job we'd clean about 25 blankets, quilts, rugs, and the like. They had 173. A normal household population of knickknacks and figurines might be 150-200; they had 7,000. We used a chemical "dry sponge" on every rug and figurine.

The job went on forever, and the longer it went, the more the owners (especially the woman of the house) complained and the more additional stuff appeared. I'd have sworn they were shipping it in. But she knew every piece and had a story to go with it. I believe every single man working on that job vowed to never marry after this experience. The rest of us were more grateful than ever for whom we'd married!

In retrospect, I think I owe that couple for the insight and inspiration to start writing books on clutter.

I had been taught by my parents and grandparents that charging too much for your services was a sin, right in there with stealing, so I always bid jobs at a bare, fair minimum. Thus the only option we had was to learn efficiency: work harder, faster, and longer hours, which I did for more than fifty years, and in fact I am still doing it. I found that other peoples' attitudes were not as conservative as mine; most saw good pay for less work as the ideal. I remember hiring a college student once who needed a job. After two weeks (he was cleaning a bank) he came to me and said he wasn't happy with his new job. His answer to my "Why?" was a classic. "Because work takes up all of my time on the job," he said. "What!?" I said—I didn't understand. "Well, work takes up all my time on the job. My friend has a good job at college. He has to read a gauge for five minutes every hour, and the rest of the time he can rest and study, and get paid for all of the time he is there." The student left that day still looking for a no-work job.

> Work for hire means "work." Make sure new employees understand they aren't being paid for just showing up each day!

Scooped!

> While we are resting on our laurels, a hungry new competitor is usually casing out our comfy seat.

Six years of intense service in the city and area of Pocatello left us rather dominant in the field of cleaning. In fact, so well known was the name Varsity in cleaning that sometimes we benefited from other people's accomplishments.

The president of a big savings and loan in Pocatello was a friend of mine. He sent me and my family an invitation to watch the big Fourth of July parade from his air-conditioned second-floor office. It had a twelve-foot-wide window that directly overlooked the parade route (probably better than the Governor's view of it). I was pretty puffed up about this prestigious seating, far above the other lowly spectators crowded together out on the hot street. It was glorious to sit in a big plush corporate chair with a cool lemonade and watch the passing exhibits (in Idaho parades then, everyone rode a horse, even the twirlers).

My feeling that I had arrived evaporated as the parade neared the end. I could hear loud cheering and clapping, and knew something great was coming. I had a competitor, Jon

Bell, a twenty-year-old whose new cleaning company dared to intrude on my territory—the town where I figured I was the cleaning king. I assumed he wasn't in my league and had ignored him until now. But here at the very end of the parade he was, with several of his employees in bright yellow jump-suits emblazoned "Bannock Cleaning—we clean everything" and armed with wheelbarrows, shovels, and brooms. They were cleaning up all of the horse manure from the parade, singing as they scooped and swept. Then a last person would spray the soiled place with scented disinfectant. It was a brilliant idea, an unmatchable marketing ploy, that had the crowd not just cheering but throwing the candy distributed by earlier parade entries back to my competitor.

And there I sat, formerly fat and content, turning pale now. "What's the matter, Dad?" one of the kids asked me. "Be quiet!" I snapped. I'd learned a big lesson about staying in and on the job. I kicked myself for weeks for sitting on my rump relaxed while being outcreated by a new, young competitor! I always admired old Jon for this maneuver, but such is the redeeming value of being well known that soon afterward Varsity got a letter from the mayor, thanking us for cleaning up the manure and promising us some upcoming city work!

Vanity states

The advantages of expansion are often more ego and image than economic.

When I was first in business, expanding to another town was a real heart thumper. Moving into another state was monumental. In the early sixties we lettered our trucks "Idaho-Wyoming-Utah." My little college business was operating in three states, and four would be even better. We were cleaning a telephone building in Kanab, Utah, a town almost on the border of Arizona (many a Western movie had been filmed there). Less than ten miles across the border in Arizona was a little town called Freedonia, and it had one (1) single phone booth. In order to add Arizona to the fledgling list on our panel trucks I managed to negotiate cleaning it for $1.50 per time. It easily cost us $25 in expenses to drive down there and clean it, but it did qualify us to add Arizona to the states we had conquered. Vanity! And vexation. Since it was the only booth in town, and this was a pretty rugged area, it often doubled as an emergency outhouse. So we paid dearly for the right to clean it!

My spontaneity cost me some ground at times. If something was exciting, witty, fresh, or struck me funny, I would (without forethought, malice, and sometimes good sense) go for it. I've always disliked pigeons, for instance, because the wild ones in towns or cities pooped on everything and we had to clean it up. During one job where the pigeons had been around in numbers and done a fair amount of damage, one of the crew found a dead one, still fresh and intact. On his break, he made a miniature noose and strung the pigeon up. It looked like an old-time Western lynching, and expressed our sentiments at the time.

Someone snapped a picture of this, and I put it on the front page of our company newsletter, with a caption along the lines of, "This is what we do to dirty birds."

Once that issue of our little public relations publication (called *The Scrubber's Scribe*) was out, we found that some of our best clients raised and raced pigeons. Even the president of Varsity (me!) took some heat over this.

Before you go public with a joke, make sure it's going to be funny to everyone.

Operation Pigeon Potty

If you don't really want something, you will probably get it, so be prepared.

A less controversial excerpt from *The Scrubber's Scribe*, 1974.

The story you are about to read is true—not even the names have been changed to protect the innocent.

On a nice April morning the phone rang at Varsity headquarters in Pocatello. "Don, this is Tro," the voice said. "Meet me at 138 Main at 9 A.M. tomorrow to bid a big job." So four contractors (including me) and the owner of the building involved met the next morning. The owner got a flashlight and hammer and said, "Okay, follow me!" We went up two flights of stairs into room 209 of the old hotel next door. Then we crawled out through a tiny window onto the roof above the owner's store. There was a big piece of plywood over the door to a large attic over the owner's store, which he ripped off with gusto.

Then we stepped into an almost unbelievable abode. As we stood astounded, the owner quickly leaped in front of the door so we couldn't get out while the getting was good. He told us the sad tale. "Boys, this was 'pigeon paradise' for thousands of pigeons for years, and as you can see they left their mark." The smell up here on a hot day discourages our customers, and feathers come drifting down too, so this place has got to be cleaned!" I heard a contractor mutter under his breath, "You're crazy!" The contractor I was standing next to began to stutter, and the other was in shock, but to be polite we all crunched through the dried pigeon refuse, and quickly retreated back through the window and down the stairs.

I wrote up a bid and sent it in, figuring it was high enough that it would never be accepted.

All went well for four months, and then one day I said to our Pocatello manager, "I'll be around for a few days, *so if any jobs come up, count me in." You guessed it, the pigeon job came through. Now I had two fine young men who worked with me all summer, my thirteen-year-old son Grant and a fourteen-year-old redhead named Davy Treasure. "How would you like to make a $5 bonus, boys?" Their eyes glistened with eagerness as they said "YES!" "Okay, round up two snow shovels, two scoop shovels, a hoe, a bundle of gunny sacks, a vacuum, three brooms, and a fifty-foot rope. When they had done so I presented them with a couple of respirators. "What are these for?" Davy asked. "You'll see," I said, and led the two innocent lambs up the stairs, through the window, and onto the roof. Then I shoved them into the pigeon pit, blocking the door and saying, "Have all of this out in eight hours and $5 extra will be yours!"*

Now pigeon dust poured forth and feathers flew. When the sacks were filled with pigeon poo, they were fastened to the rope and lowered, one at a time, two stories down into Don's El Camino. Where the pigeons had roosted, the droppings were twelve inches deep, level with the rafters. The two boys dauntlessly pursued their bonus. Lying exhausted on the roof after nine hours of grueling work, they were still many sacks short of victory. The job continued for days! No one would park by the El Camino. In the restaurants where the boys ate at noon, chicken was never considered.

Finally it was cleaned—walls and ceiling scraped, inches of bird droppings sanded off the sills, and all floors not just emptied but vacuumed and hosed. Then after everything was dry, a giant spray gun was hoisted up and the entire interior of the room was sprayed with a latex sealant, to eliminate any remaining odor. Any holes, crevices, or openings were also well sealed to discourage any further feathered inhabitants.

The final statistics of the job:

- *4,138 pounds of dried pigeon waste removed*
- *1 truckload of other debris (including some long-dead pigeons) hauled away*
- *Davy (a Scout with thirty merit badges) vowed to surrender his pigeon-raising badge*

- *Grant is now cooing instead of talking*
- *The skyful of pigeons hated Varsity now and performed several dive bomb attacks*

The boys didn't make their $5 bonus. However if we can get 50 of you readers to drop us a note expressing your empathy for them, we will give them a $25 bonus. Grant and Davy are perched on the rafters, depending on you!

Driving daze

Driving was nonproductive, "no pay" time, so I did it in extra hours, before or after work, often on snowy or icy roads. I seldom knew what it was like to drive fresh. I look back and wonder how I managed not to kill myself or anyone else. Fortunately, in all of those miles, I had no accidents except a few fender benders in parking lots. We'd finish or leave a job, then drive all night to another job or (while we were still in college) to an early morning class. This meant a twelve or fourteen-hour day followed by a 300-500 mile trip home. The ones I remember best were the trips home from our Grand Canyon jobs—there were not many interstate highways then and it took forever to get home (and Utah and Idaho were full of deer on the road).

I never used coffee, soda pop, or drugs to keep awake, and was the king of "wake-up" creativity when I got drowsy. Sticking your head out of the window or slapping your face was for amateurs. I learned to stop and get a bucket of snow and put it down my back, whinny like a horse, bang my head on the steering wheel, and pretend I was a tour guide. Plus, of course, singing all of Hank Williams' songs from "Your Cheating Heart" to "Jambalaya." One night I was so tired that some road signs came alive and ran across the road on their white post legs!

One evening after an eighteen-hour day at the Grand Canyon I took off for home at 9 P.M. I drove about 400 miles, and was just twenty-five miles from home but couldn't go any farther. So I pulled off onto a little turnoff road and backed into it, with the front of my car about thirty feet off the road, but facing it. Then I fell over in the front seat to sleep a bit so I could make it home. I'd just dozed off when the sound of

a diesel truck woke me. Since I'd been fighting to keep awake all night, I thought I'd fallen asleep driving, and now I saw a brightly lighted tanker truck appearing to come right at me. I'd been snoozing on the passenger side of the front seat, so when I grabbed for the steering wheel to dodge the truck, it wasn't there. That big truck was right up on me now, and in total fear I closed my eyes to die. Zoom! The truck, of course, went right by my parked car. I was fully awake now and had enough adrenaline to drive to Denver.

So stimulated was I by the event that my romantic instinct was activated and after being gone a week was anxious to see my wife Barbara, only a few miles away. I got home, crawled into bed, kissed her on the back of the neck, and asked her why she hadn't waited up for her lover the janitor's return. Barbara, a warm, enthusiastic, passionate lover, a few hours earlier had helped a neighbor woman whose car was out of gas. In the course of this, Barbara had for the first time in her life tried to siphon gasoline. Nothing until this (including cold showers) had ever been capable of dampening my husbandly intentions, but when she rolled over and whispered back, "Hi, Honey," in 88-octane breath, I decided that for this night, the trucks and cars had won and went to sleep.

Bum rap

Staying alive is part of the job, and dumb mistakes happen more often to drowsy drivers. Push your luck too far when it comes to scanting or skipping sleep, and you'll undo everything you've accomplished with all of those extra hours... and more.

Many nights I became so exhausted I pulled off the road to sleep. As I huddled in my sleeping bag, a state patrolman would often tap on the window to see if I was a murder victim. After a couple of hours of rest I was on my way home again, arriving in time for breakfast.

After one such trip I came directly to a big job at the Blackfoot Telephone Company to help the crew. I was so tired I could hardly move, but to keep face I worked with the men at a fast clip all morning stripping floors. I was unshaven and my clothes were wrinkled from sleeping in the car. At noon we all went to the city park to eat our lunches. We stretched out to take our usual ten-minute break. When the men got up to go, I couldn't move and told them I was going to rest for ten more minutes. I dozed off only to be awakened by the city police who were kicking me soundly on the bottom of my feet. "All right, you bum, get up and move along—there's no loitering in this park." My account of this thoroughly elated the men, and caused me to be more selective in both grooming and resting places.

I finally pushed my luck to the point that I quit driving when tired. In 1972, on the new interstate right outside Pocatello, for the first time ever I must have fallen asleep at the wheel, for I found myself driving off the shoulder and into a ditch. I looked to my left, and there was a state trooper driving alongside me, only he was still on the highway. He never stopped me or gave me a ticket—just looked at me, shook his head in pity, and drove on. I took this as a sign that it was time to get more rest or stay home.

CHAPTER 3

Sun Valley Surprises

We meet the elite

FOR EVERY contractor there comes the one or two "big ones;" jobs by which you either win or lose big. Our maintenance contract with Sun Valley, America's first ski resort (built in 1937), nestled in the Idaho mountains, was a flagship project for us that launched many fine new contracts afterward.

In addition to the floors, walls, desks, windows, and toilets we were now proficient in cleaning, this epic contract broke new ground, adding the multiple dimensions of "facility maintenance" to the building maintenance we were accustomed to doing. Here we were soon setting up conventions, building docks, doing landscaping, demolishing old dorms, laying fires, painting ski lifts, building fence, making snow, carving signs, installing sprinkler systems, retrieving golf balls and evicting gophers, and more. We did all of this for and in the midst of a vacation wonderland, with a rich clientele, wild winters and beautiful summers, leaving us with experiences far richer than any guest's.

The Ski Patrol

It's not what you do for a living that counts, but how you feel about it. More proof that attitude can overcome all!

It was 1970, and the famous ski resort Sun Valley at this time was owned by former Olympic skier and investor, Bill Janss. Mr. Janss had employed my janitorial firm, Varsity Contractors, to clean the resort. Our contract began in the spring. We cleaned, painted and built all manner of things to keep things looking sharp. Mr. Janss was impressed with our efforts and when winter set in, he called me into his office and said, "Don, you are a toilet cleaner, aren't you?" Proudly, I held out a disinfectant-wrinkled hand with bowl cleaner stained fingernails, said evenly, "Yes." "Well Don, in a few weeks, I'll have 5,000 skiers on that mountain and 20 toilets. Do you know what that means?" (A new contract was coming my way.) "How about it? Can you clean those toilets that are spread all over the mountain?" I assured him the job was "no problem" and I would submit a bid for the work. He accepted my bid and we now had 20 new buildings to clean.

Only four of these restrooms had water; the remaining sixteen were chemical toilets that required charging every 3-5 hours with five gallons of chemical solution hand-carried up the mountain. It wasn't difficult to train someone to do the technical parts of the job, and so much of the servicing was skiing time that you might think it was an enviable position. However, then there was the matter of social status. Who wanted to be a toilet cleaner in fashionable Sun Valley?

I would interview applicants and describe, outline, and promise until their eyes glowed with eagerness to tackle the chore. But in a few days, the social status of the position would get to them. Then they would begin to sneak around, trying not to be seen or recognized as the Varsity toilet cleaner. I raised the pay a dollar more an hour than any other cleaning position in our organization, and still had difficulty keeping the job filled for long. I set up a free lunch for them and still the image of "toilet cleaner" outweighed the attraction of the slopes and the other benefits. I was about at the end of my rope when big Bill Zickgraf appeared.

Bill was from South Carolina, 6'4" and thirty-five years old. A former All-American swimmer, state senator, and college educated, he sparkled with Southern charm. He had brought his young family to a log cabin in the mountains of Sun Valley for an experience in living in the wilds. He declined acceptance to law school to remain in the area for a while, and came to me seeking employment.

"I need some work, Don." "What kind?" "I'll do anything." My pulse pounded—I realized I had a live one. I would have to do the job again myself if I didn't get someone hired. "I've got just the job for you, Bill. You can learn to ski and you'll have a free meal." "Great, I'll take it, what is it?" I told him, and his eyes glistened with enthusiasm. "That sounds good and I really want to learn to ski. I'll be ready to start in the morning."

The story that follows is now a legend in Sun Valley. Bill rode the chairlift up and walked through all of the locations, charting his course of action. Once he had the route memorized, he strolled into a ski shop and purchased a set of skis that looked like they'd been made from giant redwoods, and a pair of boots to match. Then he got back on the ski lift, a basket of cleaning supplies neatly under each arm. He had never skied before and was headed to the top of the mountain to learn.

At the end of the first lift he had to go down a hill to the next chair lift. The slope was a small one but for a nonskier a potential disaster. Bill froze in fear as the slick skis headed down the slope to the lift hut. A small rail fence served to guide the skiers down the hill but when our gallant arrived, 215 pounds of muscle, skis, and toilet supplies, he hit it hard, causing a spectacular derailment. Toilet articles flew everywhere—urinal blocks skidded across the hard snow like hockey pucks, and rolls of toilet paper rolled down the hill, unfolding in great displays. Brushes, sponges, and other toilet articles were strung all over the place and oncoming skiers had to dodge skillfully. (Some were really amazed that they would be dodging a sliding sanitary napkin on a ski slope.) It was a hilarious sight for the skiers lined up there, and they roared with laughter. It was a moment that would have washed out any other employee, but not Zickgraf. He removed his skis, waved and laughed back at his audience, retrieved his basket of goodies, put his skis back on, and continued on.

Within three weeks there was a miracle on the mountain. Complaints about the condition of the restrooms stopped. Bill not only did a good job of cleaning, he used his spare time to develop into a fantastic skier. Furthermore, he was no longer the scoff of Sun Valley, but a widely recognized and colorful hero of the hillsides. In fact, he was the most famous man on the mountain. He hadn't let the low image of the janitor get him down. In melodramatic fashion he would seize a couple of mops, one in each hand like ski poles. Then he would push off from the highest peak and gracefully glide through the skiers. The ski school students, paying $20 an hour to learn, would all stop when Bill came by. "There he goes!" All heads would turn as Bill, handling the two mops as gracefully as a bouquet of flowers, a radiant smile on his handsome face, zipped by. There were many well-known and influential people in the ski schools. One man from the show "What's My Line?" got so excited he offered Bill an appearance on the show. "No one would guess the skiing toilet cleaner of Sun Valley, Idaho!" he said.

The first aid and safety patrol men, rugged and good-looking, usually occupied the top rung of recognition, but this toilet cleaner was stealing their thunder. The safety patrol wore bright orange coats with a big white cross on them, which identified them as the ski patrol. Bill had a picture of an old-time outhouse, moon on the door and all, silkscreened onto an attractive sweatshirt. The next day, down the hill he came, with BOWL PATROL blazed in big letters across the back and front.

Zickgraf set a precedent for service that winter, and could have written a book on his experiences. But most importantly of all, he totally reversed the status of the job. By August of the next year over a dozen people were asking for it, many of them willing to do it for nothing!

Snow removal at Sun Valley

After five years of handling snow in the Northwest for the telephone company, I figured I knew all about it. Then came Sun Valley. Amazing what a few thousand feet in elevation can do for snow depth! I have a picture of us shoveling eight feet of snow there. We were supposed to keep the paths in the condo complex plowed, and was that a no-win situation. It could snow fifteen to eighteen new inches over the night. We had efficient Toros that could blow away light snow in minutes, but the machines were noisy and irritated late sleeping guests. They paid $200 per night for a room, and screamed if we showed up at five, six, seven, or even eight or nine, so we had to wait until early risers had tromped eighteen inches of easy snow into three inches of ice cement— almost impossible to remove.

As the winter progressed, more snow accumulated—five, six, seven feet of it on the roofs, and it settled into a heavy, compact sheet about four feet deep. It was heavy enough to weigh on the doors inside the buildings, and guests got anxious when the bathroom door stuck, and the hospital people panicked when they couldn't open the operating room door. Our turn! We tried everything to scientifically remove roof snow—from loosening the base of it with a wire, to hoisting a blower up on the roof. We finally resorted to hand snow shoveling. We cut the four-foot layer of snow into 2' x 2' squares and slid it off. We charged $150 a roof. A good man could shovel a roof in a day.

I myself loved this job. Up in the crisp, pure air amidst some of the most beautiful mountains in the world. The sky a blue no artist could mix, and a perfect sun! The excuse to be there? Profit, plus a further inducement—competition. We had great roof races. Winning required iron discipline—small, careful consistent cuts and blocks and no breaks. The greedy and reckless who seemed to be winning at first paid dearly in the end. The motel I owned there, the Red Top, had steep metal roofs and a

good door slam at the right time caused a little avalanche and a perfect, free roof cleaning job. This was great if you weren't on the front porch wondering what the rumbling was above you.

While many saw avalanches only on TV, I lived in an avalanche area. One morning at 3 A.M., driving home from Boise, the conditions were perfect for it. The snow base was packed, the surface glazed hard, and tons of new snow had been dumped on the mountain over the past several days. The heavy layer of new snow slipped on the frozen layer beneath, and down the mountain it came, thousands of tons of snow, picking up pine trees, rocks, and more snow as it gained momentum. That mountain, just between Hailey and Ketchum (Sun Valley), was several hundred feet from the highway, so when the sheriff stopped me to say that the highway was closed, I figured the slide must have been up north by my home, so I could at least spend the rest of the night in the office instead of the Varsity van. So I went around the roadblock and got to see how fast an avalanche can move. It wasn't a slow rumble and tumble (they play it in slow motion on TV). At like sixty miles an hour it swooped down like a white flash. Some cars ahead of me were stranded by the slide deposit, which reached from the mountain across the road, and included not just snow but rocks, trees, tangled fence wire, etc. I couldn't miss the opportunity to jump in as a volunteer to help clear the road. Awesome what an avalanche can do!

I once was called with my old Ford tractor to take the snowmaking unit into a pavilion area to provide a blanket of white for a Bing Crosby and Ann-Margret special. Ann-Margret melted it! Our "snow jobs" were hard work, but full of adventure.

In winter, mops, brooms, and patio squeegees were replaced by snow blowers, snow shovels, ice prods, and plenty of warm clothes. Although it might appear a tough, cold job, there was color and excitement for those who braved the howling wind and subzero weather, as this letter home from one of our junior workers shows.

January 29, 1979

Dear Mom,

I arrived here to work for Varsity at nine on Friday morning. The boss, a man named Mark Browning, looked younger than me. He told me to throw my suitcases in the Boise (some former lambing sheds, now a dorm) and meet the roof crew in thirty minutes. They handed me a snow shovel, and hauled us in a four-wheel drive vehicle to the condominiums where the guests stay. Then I was ordered by this young Browning guy to climb up on the roof and shovel it off—the snow was 5 1/2 feet deep, and packed solid! Browning told me it would only take three hours. I thought he meant three hours to climb up on the roof, but I was wrong. He expected me to remove all the snow in three hours.

I was going to quit on the spot, but Browning took down the ladder and left me on that two-story roof. He told me that when I finished the snow below would be high enough that I could just step off. It was twenty-two below zero, and to survive I had to shovel like mad. The snow went fast when I learned to cut it into blocks and slide it off. If I tromped on it the snow broke into powdery granules that took forever to remove. "There must be an easier way," I yelled over to Browning (who had already cleared 3/4 of a roof by himself). "Nope," he yelled back. "We've tried wire saws, snow blowers, football players, and drunks. You're doing it—keep working!" They didn't stop for lunch, Mom, because the truck that brought us froze to the ground.

After yells of victory began coming from inside the house, I knew my job was appreciated because the doors must be working again. Smells of hot chocolate and fresh donuts drifted up to the roof, but I couldn't get down to invite myself in because my snow pile wasn't high enough. As darkness descended, Browning shouted encouraging words to help me finish, like, "You'll freeze to death if you're not done in thirty minutes!" and "Now that you're warmed up, you'll be able to shovel two roofs tomorrow." I hurried to preserve my life. With every muscle aching, and blistered hands, I stepped off my roof. Success felt good until Browning showed us 75 more units needing to be shoveled!!

Your son,
Ellis

Finding out how our predecessor did the job in question before pioneering our own approach can save us some things learned the hard way.

Once the snow quit, our call of the wild wasn't over—there were the icicles. Sunny days (which caused roof snow to melt) followed by cold evenings accumulated icicles like you wouldn't believe on the two- and three-story condos and lodges. Many icicles were eighteen inches in diameter and ten to fifteen feet long. One was three feet thick! We knew nothing about removing them except that if past contractors did it, we could find a way to do it better!

Another thing we knew nothing about is why those contractors carried big sheets of plywood on their trucks. That mystery was solved at the end of our first day on icicle duty when it was just getting dark and fifteen below zero. I was picking at the base of an enormous icicle. It came loose and at great speed struck the slanted "snow rock" (the hard mountain of snow we had shoveled off the roof during the winter), and then glanced off at even greater speed, breaking right through a huge thermopane window of the condominium, sliding across the carpet,

and stopping near the fireplace where a family was relaxing in front of the fire and hoping for a quiet evening at the resort. An impressive and expensive way to discover that windows needed to be protected when you were de-icicling.

Operation Christmas Tree

Even the fun things can usually be done a better way.

Our motto at Sun Valley was: "We can clean anything and will solve any of your maintenance problems." The Sun Valley Company gave us the opportunity to fulfill our brag by asking us to contract "Operation Christmas Tree." On December 25th every year, hundreds of guests were snuggled comfortably in the lodge to ski and enjoy a few winter days in the West. In such a short stay, a Christmas tree was hard to come by. When a guest would call for one, a carpenter or other maintenance employee would round up a tree and deliver it. This was very expensive and the company was reluctant to pass the whole cost on to the guests. In 1969, the tree project generated a $5,000 loss for the Sun Valley Company. This was a problem, and when the company approached us, we tackled it.

Bill Zickgraf, now area manager, thought over the need, talked to the registration desk, and got a list of all the guests scheduled during Christmas. He then printed up some postcards offering four and eight-foot trees, decorated or "U decorate." The cards were mailed in October and in November, Bill ordered a truckload of trees and bought rooms full of decorations wholesale. He then enticed a crew of decorators and deliverers. "Enticed" you say? Yes, enticed. After all, if you would get to deliver Robert Redford's, the Kennedy family's, James Arness', Doris Day's, or Art Linkletter's tree, what would you charge?

This is what happened. As soon as a guest arrived, starting December 18, Varsity's tree crew or local church fundraisers would decorate and deliver a tree, and what a great time they had! Our secretary, Carolyn, had to make an emergency delivery and guess who lifted her up to put the star on top? Steve McQueen! My wife and daughter delivered a tree to Gregory Peck and he came out in his bathrobe and in his very polite way said, "Hello, young ladies." It took two weeks to get my wife down out of the air.

When Christmas was over, crews would retrieve the trees, and strip off and pack and store the decorations for next year. It was a great project and guests could now celebrate the holiday without putting the Sun Valley Company in the red!

Santa's bodyguard?

When dealing with the public, expect the unexpected (and if it's an imbibing public, double that!).

Well, why not? They have Santa's helpers, don't they? Santa couldn't make it without helpers, and every once in a while he needs bodyguards, too.

Santa made an annual visit to Sun Valley. The resort furnished Santa a real sleigh and some genuine reindeer to pull him. The crowds lined up around the courtyard and railings of the Swiss-style village to greet the jolly man and his sleigh full of presents. Sun Valley furnished free hot wine and rum to everyone at this Christmas Eve event, and by the time Santa arrived on the scene, many of the children's parents had had a snort of the free liquor and were chomping at the bit to see what he might bring.

Soon, with a jingle, jingle, jingle, in all his splendor, into the courtyard Santa came. The children were squealing happily and the locally trained reindeer were doing just what they had rehearsed. All was perfect until the shoving from the back of the line pushed the people in front through the barricades, causing the line to break and scores of overexcited kids (prompted by overzealous parents) massed toward Santa. The reindeer became alarmed and wheeled and stampeded right over the top of the sled. Then those famous prancing and pawing little hooves pulverized the presents and did several unpleasant, injurious, smelly things to Santa! This shortened Santa's visit considerably, due to the need for a quick trip to the hospital.

Thus for next year's visit, Varsity was asked to provide a corps of bodyguards or find a way to get Santa into the courtyard unhurt. Varsity came up with a great plan. It was spectacular, foolproof, and the would-be Santa would do it for a $200 flat fee! One of my seasonal employees was a pre-med student and a skydiver! "Give me a Santa suit and bag of toys and I'll jump and land right in the circle—guaranteed!"

The resort people were impressed, but eyeing the pinnacle on a steeple next to the courtyard, felt the risk of a Santa shish-kebab was too great (especially after last year's stampede). So Varsity's crew and managers only got to guard the line on foot so that Santa was able to meet the kids, give out candy, and retain his life and dignity.

At Sun Valley there were always incidents and happenings that could brighten even the darkest moment. Such as the following, reported in our newsletter *The Scrubber's Scribe.*

> Being raised on a farm, I learned to work day or night, so I grew up not fearing darkness. But some of my employees got pretty nervous cleaning big buildings alone in the middle of the night, and LeRoy was one of these.
>
> He was a good worker, loyal and industrious, but a little slow on the uptake and he spooked easily. He cleaned the Sun Valley Opera House after hours, a creaky, dimly lighted old theater. It took all of his nerve to whip in there, clean, and get out. One night LeRoy was sweeping between the seats at his usual high speed, eyes shifting nervously to spot any approaching goblins or their relatives, when unbeknownst to LeRoy, the projectionist, after a late party, had slipped in the back stairs to edit a film or two for the convention in the morning. When LeRoy was about halfway through his sweeping, the lights began to slowly dim. He froze in his tracks! Then slowly the large curtains began to open with groans and squeaks. LeRoy's breath about gave out on him. Then strange sounds came from a soundtrack accidentally running at the wrong speed—the language of the goblins! LeRoy fled in terror.
>
> The next morning our manager, one of Varsity's greatest talkers, reassured LeRoy that there were no such things as spooks, gave him a magnificent new trouble light, and talked him into going reluctantly back to work again. Two of Varsity's pranksters, who had heard about the incident, decided to add to LeRoy's terror. One of them, a 6'3" California boy, made up his face as pale as a corpse, wrapped himself in a white sheet, stationed himself inside the tiny janitor closet, and waited. Soon LeRoy appeared, glancing nervously around. With his nerves on edge and heart pounding, he opened the door of the janitor closet and was paralyzed with fright as a huge gruesome form with open eyes and a glassy stare teetered stiffly and fell to the floor.

That was not LeRoy's finest hour—it was his last. We haven't found him yet to give him his 1971 W-2 form.

Among Varsity's spook stories, we find another eerie setting. The Varsity crew had to clean "Warm Springs Hut," a restaurant at the base of famous Mt. Baldy. Workers always went in pairs because of the spirit or ghost said to abide there. We had records for cleaning speeds set at the hut. One dark January night, right after our men had seen a TV episode on Bigfoot, they proceeded in a howling wind, with car doors locked, to the hut to clean it. They were so frightened that one mopped while the other stood guard, watching for any form that might emerge from the mountains. This evening Rex Turner, the manager, bundled up in a big fur coat, decided to spot check his night crew, and the hut was his first stop. Because of the wind, the two spooked men didn't hear anyone approach, and they had left the door ajar to dry the fresh floor wax. Rex slipped in the back door quietly, behind the two men watching the front, and in his big, gruff voice roared "Bigfoot!" Both men were psyched up enough to respond exactly as you'd imagine. Rex had to talk calmly for a half hour to get one off his knees, to which he had collapsed after his greeting. The other simply clutched his mop harder, and I understand his hands are still clenched around it today.

Fear of the dark and of spooky settings are not funny subjects for everyone.

Shootout on the slopes

Cooperation, competition, and camaraderie can often combine to get a nearly impossible job done.

(A report from one of my managers, Mark Browning.)

I had painted chair lifts before, and knew that it was no fun. Generally, the construction crews got everything erected just in time for the first big snowfall and the poor painters ended up coating the chairs and doing their touch-up work wallowing up to their knees in the freezing white stuff. Of course, there are nicely typed construction time-tables drawn up by gagwriters in the home office which show how everything will be done on schedule and we will all have plenty of time to get our work finished before bad weather sets in, but we all know how that goes.

As it turned out, the Cold Springs lift was no exception to this pessimistic painter's rule of thumb, and I found myself standing in the snow at the top of Cold Springs Canyon with another fool, trying to paint the chairs.

The wind was only blowing about twenty-five miles per hour that week, and the temperature was up to twenty degrees, so we had relatively good weather. The chairs were already primed and hung on the cable, and the idea was to start the lift and run them between two idiots (one of which was me) standing on the lift unloading platform with airless spray guns in their hands, Vaseline smeared on their faces, and nothing in their heads. As each chair glides by and pauses momentarily between the two goons, they begin spraying with khaki green industrial enamel. The chair gets at least a little paint on it before it moves on its way again.

The only rules in this undeclared war are that you can only spray the other guy when there is a chair between you, and the downwind man gets to switch with the upwind man every twenty-five chairs or so. I measured the paint buildup on my face one day, and it came up just under an eighth of an inch! My coveralls, by the end of that job, had over a half inch of dried paint on them, and weighed in at about thirty pounds. We also had frozen hands, frostbitten feet, and getting the truck unstuck and back down the mountain to look forward to each day.

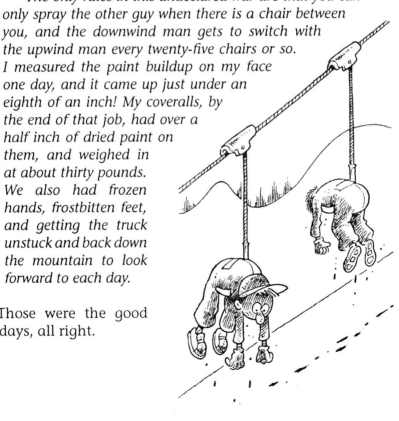

Those were the good old days, all right.

Uniform blues

Uniforms serve many good purposes, and if carefully chosen, one of the most important of these is making identity unmistakable.

We had a struggle deciding on uniforms for the company at Sun Valley. Once we all wore "whites." Linen companies would visit us and talk us into using grays, browns, yellows, and finally blues. I never did like the blues because I was often mistaken for the Pepsi man, the gas man, the postman, etc. The last straw came one evening when I was mistaken for a bus driver. Our company owned a big four-wheel drive van with three rows of seats, and with its oversized tires it could go almost anywhere. I drove it over to the elite Sun Valley Lodge one day and parked it in the "Reserved" spot in front (a janitor's privilege, by the way). I leaped out and as I came through the front door was met by a group of conventioneers who were more than slightly inebriated. "What time does the bus leave, Mac?" one asked me. "I'm not a bus driver," I said. "Hell you're not! That's the bus, isn't it?" he said, gesturing to the Varsity vehicle. "No Sir, that's a janitor crew truck."

"Come on, man, we need a bus!"

Drunks can be obnoxious, but they were guests. I finally got free of them and proceeded to complete my errand. When I returned, the truck was gone. I figured someone on our crew needed it (we always left the keys inside), but when I walked to the shop it wasn't there either. I called everyone I could think of and searched all the parking lots, but there was no sign of it.

Finally I called the Sun Valley special agent. We were cruising around in his patrol car looking for the truck when an emergency call came over the radio reporting a "tank" driving around on the sidewalks and footpaths in the condominium complex. We rushed over and there was the truck, abandoned, straddling a footbridge, not one of the four wheels touching the ground. Lined up neatly on the hood were six empty cocktail glasses. We changed our uniform color again as soon as we could after that!

Justice for the toilet thieves

Choose your stand-ins with care, and be aware before you brandish!

Although some might sneer at the dedication and commitment some of us toilet cleaners have, this seldom dampens the spirit of a true cleaner. I guess from the other side of the picture it might appear amusing at times to see and hear someone baring their soul about the fine art of sanitizing a toilet. Such was the case one afternoon when I had been employed to teach a group of resort hotel housemen and maids the fine art of cleaning a restroom properly. The group consisted of one or two old pros, and all the rest were college-age young men and women whose interest in hotel cleaning was strictly "get by," so that they could qualify for a free ski pass and the other social advantages this particular job gave them.

They were good All-American kids and found my dead-serious presentation on the subject pretty humorous. The more I preached on the precious art of getting under the toilet lid just right and polishing the chrome of the flush lever, the more I entertained them, and soon they were in fits of laughter: "Oh, man, can you believe this?... he's got to be kidding!" Remembering my own college days, I began (as I got into the more serious business of disinfecting the trashcans) to see the humor of it from their point of view. In fact, it even started to sound funny to me.

Then a stroke of fate brought an early and welcome end to the session. I'd brought my kit of demonstration equipment and visual aids with me to the class, including Johnny mops, brushes, spray bottles, rubber gloves, "Keep Out" signs, etc. When I left the room for a minute to get some more chalk, some pranksters in the group hid my case of visual aids. I knew by the smirk on their faces what they had done, though they were trying to look innocent. Not even the manager of the hotel could get them to fess up.

Determined not to proceed without my tools of demonstration, I rushed to the nearest janitor closet and got the few things I needed, including another Johnny mop, tucked the same as mine into a handy carrying cradle. These were all used items, however, and the Johnny mop, instead of being a new, dry, half-ounce of cotton, had been left by the last cleaner still soaked with bowl cleaner. I didn't realize this until I was at the climax of my description of the proper way to clean a toilet. I seized the mop and whipped it in the air enthusiastically over the group. The sopping wet blob of cotton sprayed the caustic acid bowl cleaner all over the group, especially the jerks in the front row who hid my kit. Luckily no one got it in their eyes, but plenty of damage was done to all of the expensive ski sweaters, leather jackets, and other clothing that the acid hit. This was one of the most dramatic dismissals of nonbelievers I ever witnessed, and a real stroke of justice for a band of toilet supply thieves.

When our Sun Valley operation was at its peak, not only were we doing most of the janitorial maintenance and cleaning in the area, we were also doing the majority of the grounds maintenance. The crew that handled these jobs were called "Outside Varsity" and one month we had a unique group of jobs in progress. One was building a barbed wire fence four miles long for a rich rancher from New York. On that job we cleared timber, moved rocks, removed old buildings, erected large gates, and surveyed fencelines alongside the beautiful Wood River.

The fence job provided us with some memorable moments. While dragging some cottonwood trees out of the way, for instance, an unnoticed hive was ripped apart and the angry bees decided to avenge their disturbance. They circled into attack formation and then proceeded to pursue our crew. I yelled for everyone to freeze, but men scattered in every direction. One of them, a California city boy, had never been stung by a bee in his life. I caught view of him headed for the river at a dead run. He had taken his shirt off and was waving it and swatting like a madman, attracting more bees with each movement. The man running the tractor that had hit the hive leaped off and headed out also, leaving the tractor in gear. It went down the expensive row of newly planted posts, knocking them all down like a row of dominoes. Looking back and seeing the tractor in its wake of destruction, he ran back into the bees and mounted the tractor to bring it to a stop. To this day the tractor carries the scars of the "great bee attack."

I sat quietly on the ground the whole time and was not stung once. Within thirty minutes both the bees and the boys were back to work.

Making a beeline isn't always the best approach.

One of my part-time employees at Sun Valley was the on-call ambulance driver, and often had the ambulance with him, even on a cleaning job. The name of the game was not to be on the same job with him when he got a call, because their code is that two people are better than one, so he would grab whom-ever and away they would go.

I was the whomever one day. His emergency pager went off and he was delighted that his big boss was the only person at hand to show off for. The guy was crazy—he loved to drive fast (I think that was the only reason he took the job), and with the siren and red light he didn't have to honor any traffic rules. We skidded into a low-income housing alley. The police were already there and people were wildly signaling us. I had no idea what to do, so I grabbed the other end of a gurney and we ran into the house. Kids were screaming, and the adults were wailing, "Ohhh no no, oh no." There, lying unconscious, was a woman of about thirty-five. I heard someone say, "Overdose," and then everyone cleared away from her, even the police and the ambulance driver. Everyone was looking at me and wait-ing for me to do something—I was a big boss in the area and serving as a lay clergyman at a local church, so I guess they figured I knew what to do with a half-naked unconscious (or dead) person. I had no idea where to grab her to roll her onto the gurney, but somehow did it.

On the way to the hospital he left me in the back of the ambulance with an unfastened gurney and then drove up that 25-mph speed limit stretch of road between Ketchum and Sun Valley over ninety miles an hour, cornering that big panel wag-on like a Porsche. I had my arm around her and the gurney, and she woke up, looked at the grubby janitor next to her, and (probably fearing for her life on this suicide ride) passed out again. I drove a school bus once and one year was enough, and one trip, for the ambulance, did it this time.

Expect the unexpected—cleaners are often asked
to fill other roles as the situation demands.

Salt Lake City shocker

Moving and transporting things is the best way to damage both them and nearby things, as well as who knows what else. Pack carefully, cushion and balance your loads, and use one more rope, cord, knot, or bungee cord than you think you need.

A typical "Varsity marathon" occurred midsummer in 1972. I was up at 6 A.M. and had my corporate duties done by 10 A.M. I quickly changed clothes and headed out to the mansion belonging to Bill Janss (the owner of Sun Valley Ski Resort) to complete a volleyball court I was building there. He'd picked an old creek bed for the purpose and there was only one cup of dirt for every truckload of boulders. I was on a deadline and picked rocks and leveled with my tractor until 8 o'clock that evening. I took a break then to watch a seven-pound rainbow trout jump in Bill's private lake, but forgot to eat. I rushed back to the office for a staff meeting, and one of the managers there reminded me that we'd promised to paint the kitchen of the Hawkes' cabin that evening as a favor to a retired rancher and his wife.

We loaded the paint and equipment and drove through the pines to the old cabin, built in the 1800s. Two hours later we had the job done and received a big piece of apple pie baked in a woodburning stove. It was midnight, and I ached for the old king bed. But I'd volunteered to show a crew in Twin Falls how to seal concrete in a large wholesale grocery outlet building, and promised I'd be there tomorrow with the seal. The only available seal of this type was in Salt Lake City, 325 miles away. A delivery had failed to come through, and I also needed to pick up some material for a ballfield backstop I was building. So at 1 A.M. I left for Salt Lake City in a company utility truck.

Somehow I managed to make it there, and it took two hours to measure, buy, and load the galvanized metal pipe for the backstop. To save room I shoved the small pipes inside the larger ones, and lashed the large pipes securely to the truck rack. Then I hurried to the chemical plant and bought the seal. At 11:45 A.M. I was finished and had to be in Twin Falls by 4 P.M. to start the floor-sealing job. Not in the keenest state of mind by now for lack of sleep, I started down sloping Temple Street in the center of Salt Lake City. It was the noon rush hour, and the stoplight ahead turned red faster than I expected. Platoons of people started crossing the intersection as I hit the brakes. Like a row of rockets, the unsecured smaller pipes inside the large pipes launched out into the intersection. It was awful—the noise of those pipes banging off the truck and hitting the street at all angles, and shooting into the crowds. People were running, jumping, and dodging my barrage. Some pipes that had made it through the crowds were rolling free down the street, and some were still hanging off the truck, which looked like an octopus with rigor mortis. Anyone who hadn't run for his life was shaking a fist or glaring daggers at me, as I (unshaven, and covered with kitchen paint) jumped out to retrieve and restore my load.

Fortunately, no one was hurt and no police arrived by the time I reloaded, so I escaped from the scene of the crime and four hours later pulled up in front of the grocery warehouse where two truckloads of crew and equipment were waiting. Ten of us started prepping the concrete, and by 11:30 P.M. that night the floor was cleaned, etched, and dry, ready for the seal. The petroleum-based seals used then were very volatile and flammable, and had an offensive odor. Most people could apply seal for about two hours, and after that, the fumes (which got into your bloodstream) began to make you lightheaded.

The floors were finished at 3 A.M. and the two-hour drive home was all that was left. I stopped by the office and checked for mail and problems before heading home to catch a few winks after my sixty-hour marathon. I didn't finish up until noon and didn't get to bed until 9 P.M. that night, after dealing with some church and Scout responsibilities.

Sometimes there was just no escape from schedules like this. The work had to be done and on schedule, or else! It was tough but a challenge, and satisfying when you succeeded. The physical work never bothered me much—I loved it. It was phone calls like the one two days later from the grocery store that zoned me. "Mr. Aslett, all of our bread and cereal smells and tastes like cool!" It seems the fumes were readily absorbed by grain products, right through the packaging, and nothing could be done but dispose of it all. Fortunately the grocery people had picked the seal so they absorbed the loss.

Our grocery store inflictions didn't end with wiping out the carbohydrate inventory. A few months later, we were cleaning in one of the big chain stores (Albertson's), and our crew was using a strong ammoniated chemical to strip the floor, the fumes of which withered every exposed vegetable in the whole produce department.

Alley oops!

Fumes may be invisible but they can be potent and even deadly—stay aware.

We had learned by now that drinking a quart of milk before applying seal would give you some resistance to getting dizzy, sick, or high on the fumes. But the lacquer-base seal they used on bowling alleys was like the difference between drinking lite beer and 100-proof liquor. I've never tasted an alcoholic beverage of any kind, so drunkenness was not among my experiences, but unknowingly I experienced a close second.

The bowling lanes in American Falls, Idaho, had just been refinished by some traveling pros, and the owner called us to come in that evening and help shampoo the carpet and clean the kitchen before the reopening. So several of the Varsity guys and the owner of the lanes all went to work. The refinisher had told the owner to close the windows to keep dust out, so it was stuffy in there. Your eyes started to sting the minute you entered the building, and the smell almost knocked you over.

After an hour, we were all having a good time and joking— even the normally quiet and serious owner was giggling. I just figured the job was going so well we were all in a good mood, until I tried to go up a stepladder and missed the step. My legs just wouldn't go where I wanted them to, so I stepped again, and missed. "Gadfrey, I've got polio," I thought, "or the dumb ladder is dodging me." I didn't seem very coordinated, nor was anyone else there at this point. Some of the crew were staggering and missing parts of the carpet, and the cleaners closest to the lanes were singing like lovesick wolves.

Someone finally announced that we all needed fresh air. Driving home was almost an impossibility, and even in the cool Idaho mountain air it took a while to sober up.

Only a week later, the lanes in the bowling alley at Ketchum were refinished. The owner came in the next morning and flicked on the light and the tiny spark from the light switch ignited the fumes that had built up over the night. The roof was blown off in the explosion that followed and in minutes the building burned to the ground. The owner was blown clear of the fire, and he lived! Assuring proper ventilation on all jobs became company policy after this.

Varsity's training goes to the dogs

Don't give the hardest job to the newest man or woman. Or ask employees to do something you would never do.

One of Varsity's most memorable introductions of new employees happened in 1972 when Bill Zickgraf received a call that there was a foul odor in the employee cafeteria. Assuring

Bill it wasn't the food, the caller indicated that the smell seemed to originate under the floor of the old Quonset-type building. Bill promised that Varsity would take care of the problem and decided to run over and check it out. Following the smell to its most intense area, Bill spied a trap door in the floor and raising it up to investigate, was hit by the ghastly odor of a decomposing dead dog. The critter had apparently occupied the spot for months over the frozen winter, but springtime thawing had now accelerated the decay.

Quickly slamming the door, gasping for air and sickened by the sight, Bill returned to the office to find a young man seeking a job.

Bill, needing a man anyway, interviewed and hired the fellow on the spot, informing him that his services would start immediately with removing an odor from the cafeteria. Bill led the eager new employee to the trap door and handed him a rubber glove and a plastic garbage bag. Bill then carefully explained the strategy. "There is an old dead dog on the ground under this door. I want to you put the rubber glove on your right hand, hold the bag in your left, and take a deep breath. I'll quickly open the trap door and you'll jump down into the hole, grab the dog by its back leg, stuff it in the bag, close the bag, and hand it out to me. Then jump out quick before taking a breath."

The young man, anxious to perform well in his first Varsity assignment, sucked in a big breath. Bill whipped open the trap door and down into the crawlspace went the obedient new employee. All was going as planned until he grasped the back leg of the dog and the decaying limb separated from the rest of the carcass. This caused the employee to gasp in horror, and unable to tolerate the smell, he scrambled up and out of the trap door, minus his previously consumed lunch.

Once out of the hole, dizzy with nausea and failure, the fellow tore off the rubber glove, threw down the garbage bag, and terminated his employment on the spot. This was the shortest employee training and orientation session in Varsity history.

Sun Valley odd jobs ("Let Varsity do it!")

Being open to new challenges can build your company as well as your confidence.

By this time our presence in Sun Valley went beyond being the kings of clean. We were the demons of dirt, the cure for manure, Santa's helpers, and the deans of demolition. Every Sun Valley department from food and beverage to grounds knew Varsity was hungry and competent as odd job jockeys. We had a reputation by now with our big accounts (Sun Valley and the Bell System) that we would try anything, do anything, especially if told no one else could do it.

One of the rules of the farm I grew up on was self-reliance. If you broke it, you fixed it; if you got it stuck, you dug it out; if your fence failed, *you* rounded up the runaway stock; if the tire went flat you changed it. If you needed something and it wasn't available, you made it yourself... somehow. You didn't run to the house, part in hand, whining. Ingenuity was never an option; it was a necessity.

At the time this attitude seemed cruel (today it would probably be considered parental abuse). But after you grew up, it really came in handy. Man, were we resourceful and creative. We had a shop with an anvil, forge, grinders, and other tools, and I could rivet a broken harness, ream out a bearing, or make a replacement arm for a mower support. All of this proved beneficial in my now thriving cleaning and maintenance business.

Over the years, Sun Valley provided us with every kind of job imaginable, from removing gophers from the horse corrals and recovering golf balls out of lakes, to laying fires, painting towering ski lifts, and making snow for TV specials.

When the horse trail got too dusty, I located an old sprinkler tank on a trailer, pumped out of the creek, and watered down the road. We built boat docks, an archery range, tennis and volleyball courts, ice rink benches, and a children's day care center playground. We silk-screened signs, routered out wooden signs, and dozens of other odd jobs.

When the Sun Valley Company contemplated installing automatic sprinkler systems for lodge and inn landscaping, we jumped on it. We learned how, laid in $60,000 worth of Rainbird parts, bought a sod remover, and designed and installed the entire system. Picking up trash or pick and shovel work; we did it and loved being on the end of the shovel. Anything we didn't have or couldn't buy, or that hadn't been invented, we rigged, and there was always a silent victory dance when "it worked!"

One morning Bud Siemons, the Sun Valley operations manager, called me into his office and spread out on his desk were plans for—I kid you not—a mountain! It was an authentic practice climbing mountain, with all the ledges, chimneys, sheer scaling cliffs, outcrops, crevices and footholds, etc., you would run into on a regular climb, only these were miniaturized. "Can you build this thing, Aslett?" Well, he was asking the right man, because it was all cinder block and concrete facing, the king of all building materials as far as I was concerned. I was a good mason and would have done it free just for fun of it (I bid about that low, too).

So we built it, first laying up all the blocks, and filling the cores with concrete. Once the masonry structure was up, we wrapped it in rebar (tough steel reinforcing rods) and had a swimming pool contractor come by and shoot Gunite (liquid cement) coating on it. It covered the whole thing so well our "mountain" still looks real today. Some of the crew worked on it free for the adventure I convinced them it was, so we came out okay profitwise, too.

Another time Mr. Siemons mentioned that they needed a boat dock on the manmade lake in the middle of a new condo development. "Let us build it." "Can you?" "Sure!"

I'd spent my boyhood in the desert so I'd never seen a boat dock close up. But I did a little research, drew up and submitted a successful bid, and two days later, out of a pile of logs, with the aid of a sharp chainsaw and a few clamps and nails, there emerged a boat dock. More than three decades later now, that dock is still there.

Then there was the time we moved the boathouse. It was a wooden shed, like a small house, up in the stable area and the grounds people wanted it moved to the lake beach, about a quarter of a mile or so away. The bids to move it from professional building movers with loud diesel trucks went as high as $1600, so Mr. Siemons called us in. The building was about ten feet wide and fifteen feet long, heavy, and in an awkward place for vehicles to reach. I thought about rolling it on logs with my tractor pulling, but there would be no brakes when going downhill and I could just picture it floating on the lake instead of standing beside it. Then I remembered that last year a large dome for a Playboy house had to be transported from the rail-yard and it was done by the chief Playboy Hugh Hefner himself, buying many cases of beer and rounding up a bevy of sturdy studs to carry it up where it had to go.

I put out a memo for all crew to be at the stable at 5:30 P.M., in full white uniform (for pictures, of course). I bought a case of root beer, and gave the pep talk. We surrounded the shack, picked it up pallbearer style from its slab foundation, and like a giant white-legged centipede, we propelled that thing through the pasture, down the hill, down the road, and set it on the beach. It was so much fun beating out the pros and engineers, etc., that we never billed them a penny for it. (Pure pride, I guess, but I thought it was class.)

It's amazing how much can still be done well—
and even more efficiently—"by hand."

The bishop looks bad

Another of those situations where you need to follow the wise advice: "Never explain—your friends don't need it and your enemies won't believe you anyway."

As president and owner of a big and aggressive company in a fast-paced resort town, I was competing daily for bids, dealing with employees, managers, and guests, hiring and firing, promoting and demoting. I was in charge, responsible for the company's survival.

When called to be the local man of the cloth (lay minister, or "bishop") for the Mormon church in the area, I assumed another level of expectation: always appearing to be blameless. I worked to live that way anyway, but once officially targeted with that position, many volunteered to help me stay on course, especially the managers who proudly labeled themselves "sinners." They were all decent guys who made sure I was aware of their drinking, carousing, card games, gambling, and other renegading adventures.

My very worst hour (actually few minutes) came on a Sunday afternoon. Our morning church service had gone off without a hitch. There was a large convention of insurance agents at the resort, more than two hundred of them active church members who attended the services that morning. It was a real "glory day" for me. I was in my thirties, owner of a well-respected business, had a sharp group of teachers and speakers that morning, a great spiritual lesson, and record attendance. The adult class, shaking my hand as they left, made it clear how impressed they were. I felt second to no spiritual leader in the world. I took care of a few brief items of business, closed things up, and before going home had to run up to the Challenger Inn at the resort and sign some papers.

As I entered the inn, all two hundred plus visitors to our congregation were at my left, lined up at the buffet. They thanked me, the young bishop, again for such a wonderful morning at church. Right then through the lobby came Ray Cox, head of food and beverage at the resort, and his wife Sharon. They were less active members of the church, and I had visited them several times to invite them to services.

Ray was his usual in-control, sparkling-eyed, whimsical self, but Sharon had been sampling the free wine at a Sunday morning lawn dart tournament, and was clearly under the influence. She was also without a doubt physically gifted, a fact that was not concealed by the short shorts and skimpy halter top she wore. When she spotted me, she yelled across the room, "Well it's the Bisss...shop!" Every head turned as she ran up to me and wrapped her arms and nearly naked body around me. I was trying to gently disengage her arms from my neck when loudly again, she said, "Ah, come on, Bishop, you're a lot friendlier when you come to visit me." I made a sick glance to my left and all 250 mouths were agape. Ray thought it was hilarious, and I was too stunned to be humiliated.

Vanity engineering

There were many reruns of this "filter system" scenario over the 50 years of building my businesses. The lesson here that we entrepreneurs live by is that there is no magic hand to help heal or salvage the projects you conceive. Endurance (or persistence) is the #1 requirement for survival and success.

During our surge of successes, my confidence soared. I convinced myself that my company could do anything and everything others couldn't or wouldn't.

About then I heard that the famous and beautiful Sun Valley Golf Course was struggling with a serious irrigation problem. It seemed that when water was pumped from nearby crystal-clear Trail Creek to water the greens, algae and other fine debris was constantly plugging the sprinkler heads, driving the course maintenance department crazy. It was decided a golf course filtering system was needed. Two well-known consulting engineers were called in, and they estimated that designing a filter system to strain the water would cost $30,000; to build it even more. The Sun Valley folks said "ridiculous," and sent the consultants home.

Since I had previously solved two other minor watering problems around the lodge, I asked if I could tackle the task.

Since I was a janitor, not an engineer, it took some convincing to finally get a yes. I rushed to our drafting table and drew up an impressive concrete bypass baffle system. I had worked with enough head gates, dams, and canal disbursement arrangements on the irrigation system of the ranch I was raised on that I figured my idea would work—a no-maintenance, self-cleaning, self-flushing, all-concrete filtering system.

I showed Mr. Siemons my plan, and his eyebrows raised in what I hoped was admiration. It looked so impressive I bid it for $2000 installed. They looked at my illustration of orifices, regulators, screens, and pipes, and the price, and were convinced they had nothing to lose. "Go ahead!" What a day! Would I show them!

My fine filtering system was strategically located by a rushing tributary of the ice-cold, roaring creek. I bladed out the area with my tractor, used a transit to get it level (I'd learned how to do this from my dad, who'd been a road construction foreman), and then began constructing forms. It looked so simple in my masterful blueprint, but was far harder to construct. All ten of my fingers were cut, mashed, and sprained before I was through, but I was a man on fire. The Sun Valley management was counting on me, and Bob Hope was coming to play at the course. The fate of all this rested in my hands, the Sultan of Shine, soon to be Father of Filtration.

Harry Holmes, the cool, in-control general manager of the whole Sun Valley complex, passed me every evening on his jog around the course. He ran in place for a few minutes as he passed this new memorial rising out of the ground (and just half a mile from the memorial bust of Ernest Hemingway, too).

Once the steel was in, the concrete poured, forms stripped away, it looked just like my drawing! I installed the gate and laid in the exit pipe, putting a filtering screen with round holes in it. This was a stroke of genius on my part, I thought, because the standard square-mesh screens normally used offered thousands of tiny corners to catch debris—mine didn't. As the big launch day drew near, Mr. Holmes, now really intrigued with this one-of-a-kind stack of concrete, actually stopped jogging and stared. Did I have the attention of the valley, or what?

When the first big test finally came, and the gushing force of the entire stream was loosed upon it, to me it was like opening the locks for the first time on the Panama Canal—perfect! Except, I had counted on the water that passed through the channel to self-clean the big ten-foot screen, but this wasn't quite working, so eventually the screen plugged up. Three weeks of grueling work, I had already spent well past my $2000 bid, and it didn't work! So I tinkered, adjusted, and rechanneled.

Those were black evenings as after other jobs I'd go out to the unit and wade waist deep in the icy water, hoping to spot an answer or work a miracle. This was a highly visible project and I didn't want it to be the one that fell below par. The filter system was ingenious and it would work if I had to add my very blood to the water flow to make it work. For five nights, dead tired after twelve hours of other work, I drove out to the "bomb" site to think, reason, and brood. Every night the CEO of Sun Valley jogged by with a polite wave, which only further committed me to that twenty tons of cement and engineering feat I had created. I had to get the passing water to hit the screen all over, on the edges as well as the middle. I was despairing until late one night I stuck my shovel down in the water rushing by the screen to wash the mud off of it. I turned the shovel and like a fin or rudder on a boat it kicked the water up against the screen and neatly flooded all of the moss and algae off downstream. Bingo! I had it! A series of fins along the channel designed to throw water against the screen evenly.

With shaking fingers I measured and sketched six fins. I was on the doorstep of the metal shop at 7 the next morning, and by 10 A.M. my fins were made. I clamped them on and adjusted them and... bonanza! Smoother than a Swiss watch, totally automatic, no electricity, no chemicals, no maintenance— the famous Sun Valley Golf Course had clean water at last. They were awed. I had lost money (probably $5000), suffered physically, and been ribbed plenty, but I had that last sigh of satisfaction. I delivered something better for $2000 than those engineers could for $50,000. Fifteen years later I drove up to the old filter battleground and there my invention was, still in use, working perfectly. I probably saved them several hundred thousand dollars. I only hope it gurgled, "I told you so, I told you so," every time Harry Holmes jogged by.

CHAPTER 4

For Whom the Bell Tolls: Adventures with the World's Largest Company

ONE MORNING while I was in one of my college classes, my wife took a phone call from a project manager for Western Electric, a subsidiary of Bell Telephone, asking us to bid the cleaning of a new telephone building in town. It was a $75 a week contract, the first ever of Bell's 30,000 buildings to be cleaned by an outside contractor. Bell required new disciplines in safety, security, and dust control that challenged us at first. We developed new cleaning systems to meet their standards and forged a relationship with communication companies that has lasted 50 years.

I received a $25 check—my first writing income—in 1975 from an article published in *Telephony* (a telephone industry publication). That $25 expanded into several hundred thousand dollars when an executive in charge of physical facility maintenance at AT&T headquarters in New York read it and invited me East for an interview. This resulted in me doing more than sixty two-day seminars for Bell across the U.S. I soon found that giving high-powered presentations all day was tougher than stripping floors.

These seminars was like a giant sales call for Varsity and myself, resulting in the acquisition of many more telephone company cleaning contracts and maintenance-freeing design consulting jobs for some of their major new buildings. We did a lot for, and learned a lot from, one of the greatest companies ever, The Bell System—nothing like it! (Too bad the bureaucrats broke it up!) Today we service thousands of telephone facilities across the country and are still having adventures with phone companies.

The big switchover

On important jobs, especially, the information chain needs to reach all the way down to the rank and file.

One of the most spectacular capers we inadvertently were the culprit (or victim) of was the great "early switchover." In the 1950s hundreds of telephone buildings were changed over from the old "Number, please" and rotary dialing to the new, faster ESS (Electronic Switching System). The Western Electric people would build a new facility, set up and install the much more efficient new system, and then it was turned over to the local Bell operation to switch over. This was done at midnight in a real ceremony where officials from AT&T headquarters in New York even came to participate. The switchover was simple— yank out the old wires that hung from the ceiling and dangled to the floor, and at precisely midnight the mayor of the city and other local dignitaries would be there (as when launching a new ship) to do this.

For this special occasion Bell had our crews all over the place spit-polishing anything that didn't move, and white-shirted supervisors and guests were milling all through the building in anticipation. We were just finishing up at 10 P.M., ready to go home and hit the schoolbooks, and one of my cleaners (working on his master's degree) was sweeping up the last clippings around the freshly installed block of wires for the new system. Somehow the special Bell System broom we were required to use got tangled in the wires to be yanked, and being a young, impatient fellow, seeing no harm in getting rid of some ugly dangling wires, he gave his tangled broom a good tug and pulled out half the block, instantly putting half the city on dial tone. Lights blinked, bells sounded, and it took only fifteen seconds for the head honcho to burst through the door and see the dislodged blocks. He was so upset the blood vessels on his neck were bulging. "We waited for this event for two years!" he sputtered, "and a stupid janitor has switched over the system!"

Well, they couldn't put the blocks back. So we went home in dishonor—yet with a unique honor. That was the first Bell System building in the world to go to contract cleaning, and also the only Bell office to have the big switchover done by a janitor!

How I made a million... yanking phones

While-you're-there-anyway services can be very cost-efficient.

The local Bell manager, Les Hodge, was the most progressive manager I'd ever met, next to my father. He was a risk-taking renegade in what was usually a conservative position, and when and if anything could be improved upon, Les was the first to put his name and job on the line to do it. We eventually patterned many of our Varsity systems after things we learned from him and others in the Bell System.

We had now done varied contracting for Bell for four years, and he had us doing jobs we had never dreamed of doing. We were cleaning telephone booths, phone buildings large and small, washing trucks, sealing concrete, killing weeds, cleaning equipment, painting towers, cleaning storage batteries, changing filters, removing snow, and more. In the phone company the performance of executives like Les was measured by an "index," and by now he led the entire Bell System (yes, right here in Pocatello, Idaho). We had visitors and calls from all over the country asking how he did it.

Our willingness to do all kinds of work for the telephone company brought us all kinds of jobs. One day Les asked me if we were interested in "picking up phones." It sounded like it might be worth adding to our growing list of skills, so I said we would. He explained that when people moved from a residence or business the phones (which in those days belonged to the phone company) were left behind and had to be removed and brought to the work center for cleaning and refurbishing. The usual procedure was to have telephone repairmen or installers pick them up, if they were in the area or not busy. The business of getting keys and access to the empty buildings often meant costly delays and thus the cost for each phone removed was steep—at least $5 a phone. Since we were often in buildings like this cleaning, it would be easy to just pull the phones while we were there. He offered us fifty cents a phone. It wasn't much, but usually added up to a couple extra bucks per building.

As a result of this new venture, the local telephone supervisor's cost for phone removal dropped unbelievably. Everyone wondered why, but we were doing the job on the sly because it was a union job and some unions don't understand things like efficiency and accelerated production. Since we cleaned the storeroom the phones had to be taken to, we just left behind a bag of collected phones each night. When the staff arrived the next morning, they never knew where the phones came from.

The mysteriously appearing bags of phones even became a topic of conversation at telephone company headquarters in adjoining states. Someone said it was taxi drivers that were doing the sneaky deed, so they were watched, but to no avail (they had, however, sometimes done the job before us). Finally someone in accounting scratched his head and wondered why the local janitor company was billing for removing phones, and the jig was up!

New heights with Bell

*Proving you can do something against all odds
usually precedes the more sober decision of whether
or not you actually want to do it.*

I loved working for Les Hodge; life was always exciting—
sometimes too exciting!

Early one morning some of my crew and I were shaping
up the shop we rented, when there was an anxious honking
at the door. We opened it and in drove Les Hodge, in a telephone ladder truck. He jumped out and yelled, "Close the door,
fast!" He informed us he had just driven this new truck off of
a railroad car (it didn't even have a license plate yet or a Bell
logo). He had a special project in mind and needed the truck
a few hours to pull it off, then he would take the truck to the
company garage.

The project, called "cable coating," proved to be an adventure. Long before the modern wireless transmission, the phone
company ran cable that carried all phone messages. This cable,
referred to as "bird wire," was sturdy stuff, but as it aged (and
was rubbed by tree branches, assailed by the weather, chewed
by squirrels, hit by the shotguns of pheasant hunters, etc.) some
of the insulation was damaged or wore off. This left parts of the
wire bare, and when it rained, you would sometimes lose your
connection or get static on the line. Loss of service or complaints
were things telephone companies dreaded and paid dearly for.

Most of Les' area was rural and every rainstorm or blizzard
resulted in more cases of trouble than he wanted, so he did
some research and found a plastic-like coating called Insulite
that when applied to the cable would seal up little holes and
blemishes. He had ordered a 55-gallon drum of it and since the
cable was up in the air, had commandeered the not-yet-deliv-
ered bucket truck, and you don't have to guess who he selected
for its maiden voyage—Varsity.

I was quick to suggest that we get a big padded cotton
painter's mitt, dip it in the coating, and rub it on the line as we
drove the bucket truck along under the phone and power lines.
That was good enough for Les and within an hour we were
parked under the start of the three miles of damaged cable with
the history of the most trouble. None of us had a clue as to how

to run the hydraulic bucket on the truck, but we strapped Arlo in it, pushed the buttons, and up, up, up he went. As soon as he reached the line, he dipped the mitt in the bucket of Insulite and slid the mitt along the cable. Les crept along under the cable with the truck, with me coaching from the back and trying to operate controls I knew little about, and Arlo trying to get as much of the sticky, syrupy substance as he could on the line.

We pinned him against the cross arms of telephone poles a couple of times, but by the end of the stretch no one was dead or injured, and Arlo and the truck were covered with the plastic coating (ghastly smelling stuff). Then we all went home and tried to clean off the coating. I never did learn what the construction crew had to say when they got their new truck back with what looked like splotches of varnish all over it. We waited for the next big rainstorm in that area. It came and... zero cases of trouble (whereas after the last storm there were fourteen). It worked!

Now Les was really enthused and offered us miles and miles of line coating, and we invented a brilliant line-coating machine made of spray heads, lambswool pads, and pulleys attached to an aluminum frame, which we mounted on a 25-foot long pole. We set the contraption on the line, fed the Insulite up under pressure, and walked along under the cable coating it. Les furnished the Insulite and paid us $100 a mile.

Applying this stuff was the meanest, toughest job you could imagine. The telephone lines ran everywhere, and we had to follow them. The cable ran over thickets of willow, thorn bush, and mesquite, and we would have to hack, saw, and muscle our way beneath the line, applying the Insulite as we went. We traveled over the tops of trees and boulders, through gullies,

and where the lines went 70 feet into the air, over houses and through back yards in town, across main highways and bridges, over creeks, rivers, and lakes, through farm fields, past mean dogs and other animals. Plus it was often desert hot on the site and the coating stuck to your skin, clothes, and hair and made your eyes burn.

The worst was when word got out to the other Bell System operations. Because we had just expanded our cleaning operations into Arizona, I agreed to do an eight-mile stretch of cable though some godforsaken desert north of Phoenix. It was in the rugged hills near Prescott, Cottonwood, and the historic old mining town of Jerome. Two brothers (one a printer and the other a banker) who had just gone into business with us were anxious to come on the job and help—poor souls! I drove from Idaho to Arizona in my old faithful El Camino armed with equipment and supplies, picked them up, and we drove to the area.

It was supposed to be a three or four day job, but it lasted almost two weeks. It rained and rained, and when it didn't rain it was blisteringly hot (Idaho deserts are nothing compared to Arizona). I don't know how they ever strung cable over some of that terrain. One night after coating cable all day I couldn't get my pants off because there were so many cactus thorns stuck through them into my flesh. Everything else was hurting so bad, I hadn't even noticed that. I had many more years of suffering experience than my colleagues, and they weren't prepared for this kind of break-in experience, called "survival at any cost." My two partners were both office types and neither had ever been away from their wives for long, and after four days were moping around and threatening mutiny. One actually did leave.

We finally reached the last day, and it was a toughie. We had to go through thickets so thick water couldn't even run through them—the brush was brutal. But I was anxious to be done, too. I'd been there too long, losing money most of the time. When we reached the end of the cable, the last span arched over a 200-foot-wide pond. My partner said, "There is no way!"

"We have to find a way, or we can't complete the contract," I said. A rowboat was one solution, but that meant a three-hour trip to town. It seemed like an impossible task, and I had a whimpering, homesick helper. The pond was stale, full of weed and slimy algae, and there were some half-starved cattle hanging by the edge of it pooping all over. But the drive to get home—home, sweet home—took over good sense. I strapped the pressure tank on my back, hoisted the now 30-foot extension pole with the coating unit onto the line, and waded out into the pond. It turned out to be only chest deep, but it was far from the ole' swimming hole. I kept the unit on the cable and eventually emerged on the other side, covered with moss, bugs, snails, mud, and pondweed. My partner took one look at me and said, "I can't do this!" That was his last day.

The job was only a break-even promotion project to convince the telephone company in Arizona that we wanted their business. The only thing we convinced them of was that we were crazy.

I wouldn't do a job like this now for $5000 a mile, but hopefully it helped develop character. To keep the memory of this great experience alive, I kept the cable coating equipment and it now has a place of honor in my cleaning museum.

Hot rollers

Having or remembering only part of the instructions may be worse than not remembering or having them at all.

Bell had safety and security rules covering everything from dust to fire prevention. In some areas even a single cigarette was strictly forbidden. We bid and got a painting job in Utah in such a place. It was a busy time and none of us Varsity managers had enough crew available to do the job, so we hired a local out-of-work union painter, a crusty old fellow who looked as if he might have OD'd on paint fumes a few times somewhere in the past fifty years. He was pretty bent when we told him he couldn't smoke on this job, but he agreed to do it and soon had half of the first wall gleaming with the toxic-smelling epoxy-based enamel paint specified. Duane, our supervisor on the job, noticed some roller lint in the finished area, and asked the old painter, "Didn't you burn off your roller?" (A process whereby you light a match and quickly run it around both ends of a new roller to singe off any loose fuzz before starting to paint.) The man had never heard of this, so Duane gave him a "do it next time" explanation and started to leave.

Apparently not hearing the "next time" part of the instruction, this old duffer whipped out his trusty cigarette lighter and held it under his paint-laden roller, and "PUFF!" That highly flammable paint burst into flames. In a panic, the surprised painter tried to put it out by rolling at great speed on an unpainted wall, which gave him a two-foot blazing torch at the end of an extension roller handle. In the smoke and confusion that followed, no one remembered how the fire was extinguished, nor what explanation was offered when the telephone people in the building smelled smoke.

In every telephone building there was a "power room," generally the basement, and it contained an enormous car-sized diesel generator—HUGE—timed to kick in the second municipal electricity failed so no one would lose phone service. Extending out from it, up near the ceiling, were exposed thick copper bars connected to the battery of the generator and carrying megavolts of electricity. They were harmless as they were, but when shorted (accidentally connected with each other), they would melt a wrench laid across them.

One day one of our new employees who was painting the ceiling, unaware of all this, set a gallon can of paint down on two of them. Boom!—modern art! The ceiling and everything else nearby was suddenly painted.

Give me a break!

On the ranch I was raised on, a day had only three events: starting time, noon, and quitting time. We got up at five, milked the cows at six, went to the bathroom once, and that was it until noon. At noon we often ate in the field, and sometimes without even turning the tractor motor off, because it was too hard to restart. Then work again until dark. Adjusting this lifetime of habit to fit modern office customs took some doing.

I was putting on one of my first Bell seminars, for thirty telephone executives assembled in a swanky meeting room. I started at 8 A.M. promptly, ripping into the subject with visuals and facts that created audible gasps and applause. I usually teach with an intensity that doesn't lose audiences, but at about 9:30 A.M. I noticed nervous glances at wristwatches, squirming, eye-rolling, leg-crossing, and other strange movements in the group. So I cranked my speed up another notch and laid it on thicker and faster. By 10 o'clock the whole room seemed in twitching turmoil and finally a big burly guy in the back leaped to his feet and yelled, "Let us go!" "Go where?" I asked. "To the bathroom," came the chorus back.

I said, "Well, okay," and dismissed them for ten minutes, and no stampede of alarmed cattle could have equaled the surge through that door to the restrooms. I'd never seen anything like this before. Back home on the farm we used the restroom about once a day.

In the middle of the afternoon session, 1-5 P.M., I sensed another uprising brewing and asked, "Do you people have to go *again*?" They erupted like the Mormon Tabernacle Choir on the last hallelujah verse.

At the end of the day, the head guys called me aside and explained the birds and bees of breaks in their company. I'd never heard of a "break," and not being a coffee drinker or one who stayed up half the night boozing, I didn't have a clue that

people often used the bathroom several times a day! After this I reluctantly made breaks a part of my seminar schedules.

Another memorable seminar experience was set in motion when a telephone company manager who had attended one of my earlier seminars, Horace Hosback, called and scheduled a seminar for all second and third level managers of Bell of Pennsylvania. These were some pretty high-powered conferees and this was a great opportunity. Horace presided and introduced me, guaranteeing the attendees that I'd keep them on the edge of their seats for the next two days. He also pointed out that everywhere I conducted a seminar, an exceptional event had occurred. In Miami, it had snowed, while in Milwaukee the lake froze the next week and caused a city water shortage. In Chicago the next week it got to a minus sixty chill factor, in Atlanta they had a record flood, and so on.

Not to disappoint them, the chain of events continued right there at that Hilton airport hotel. In midafternoon of the second day of the seminar, I was behind the lectern explaining the indirect cost savings in bidding, and doing so in stocking feet because the new $40 shoes I'd bought were killing my feet. (I'd always bought $12.95ers before.) Directly to the right of me was a large set of swinging doors that led into the kitchen. Suddenly there was a shattering crash from the kitchen and a female voice screamed, "Help—please! Help, police!" Some dude with a long, ugly knife knew the kitchen crew had just cashed their paychecks, and what was going on behind the doors was an armed robbery. In the process someone dropped a large tray of dishes.

The woman's second cry brought thirty-one of us leaping over tables and bursting through the door to the rescue. The crook had left his getaway car idling outside the hotel's back entrance. Pursued by a posse of one bellboy, thirty telephone managers, and one seminar teacher with his shoes on the wrong feet, the thief dove past his car into the nearby thick foliage, leaped a six-foot fence, and was swallowed up by the forest. His pursuers stopped at the fence panting like a pack of hounds, as the crook escaped. This event kept my record going, and pleased Hos and the other telephone men so much that I was able to finish and dismiss all an hour early.

The importance of orientation

The greatest and most needed program in the world can be valueless, or even detrimental, without proper orientation.

When I was working with AT&T in the New York area they had joined forces with an environmental organization in a recycling program, and had some classy paper holders made in which different types of recyclable paper could be placed, instead of being thrown in the wastebasket with the other trash. The janitors were all instructed carefully in the details of this new waste paper handling system.

One Monday morning the sharp white holders appeared on every one of the hundreds of desks in the building. The occupants of the desks, not oriented or introduced to the program yet, quickly found the perfect use for the important-looking new container—a place to put their "urgent" documents and papers. By the next morning, pounds and pounds of important and valuable documents, notes, plans, and other papers had been shredded.

Vegetable visual aids

In the world of work, at least, getting genuinely caught up in what you are doing is more important in the long run than comporting yourself elegantly. As Norman Vincent Peale used to say, "Enthusiasm makes the difference!"

My exuberance (and lack of couth in fancy settings) was always a tempting target for my fellow managers, as this essay by Dave Miller of Varsity of the South shows.

Viewing Aslett's table manners, being a Southern gentleman, I am somewhat less than inspired. On my first dinner with him, we attended one of Miami's finest eating establishments as guests of one of the Bell System's big brass, a gentleman with impeccable manners. Once we were seated and started into a formal conversation,

I glanced over in horror and saw Don violently polishing each piece of his silverware with the embroidered silk napkin. The next dinner was at an equally fine place. I had to remind Don that when one scoops or forks up some food, the next procedure is to bring the food up to the mouth, not hold the captured spoonful six inches from the plate and reach your head down to eat it. It reminded me of eating with my Irish setter.

The grand finale of Don's uninhibited eating style came in Greensboro, North Carolina, in August of 1977. We had a luncheon appointment at the beautiful Four Seasons there with the North Carolina Bell System head real estate manager, Mr. Finleyson. When we sat down to eat Don ordered his usual favorite, a fresh fruit salad. Seconds after the meal started Mr. Finleyson made the fatal mistake of asking Don a question in the area of Don's strongest opinion and enthusiasm. Don, who was sitting across from Finleyson and me, had the whole side of the table to himself to make his presentation. While eating, he gestured wildly with his fork (which contained the remains of his last bite). He slung fragments of cottage cheese everywhere as he garnered the interest of Finleyson, who managed to duck

the first projectiles. Seizing a three-quarters peeled banana like a pistol, Don pointed it at Finleyson and me, waving it right under our noses. While telling our guest how he should roll all of his maintenance needs into a single package, Don scooped the various leftovers on his plate (celery, pickle, maraschino cherry, etc.) into a leaf of lettuce, rolled it up, and munched it with one big slurping bite.

Needing a visual aid to show Finleyson one of his final points, Don turned a cup over and seizing up the place mat, ripped out a 4x4-inch section to show total coverage of the problem. Then would you believe this, needing something to demonstrate the nailing down of the idea, he reached over onto Finleyson's plate, snatched up the dinner roll, and pounded it with the ketchup bottle. I thank the Lord that I escaped from the restaurant without a fine or being struck with flying food, for I must live until another meal.

Don't bug me!

It was one of those days that could tempt a man to give in or give up. I needed money for payroll again—$2000 by the end of the week—and it just wasn't in the bank or in any immediately collectible receivable. The only hope was to pull together and do a pile of extra "route" jobs for the telephone company, which would process my billing overnight if asked.

The route spanned more than 500 miles of South Central Utah. No one really enjoyed these "must earn it" marathons, or found it easy to leave for five days. But I packed my tools, paint, ladders, and sleeping bag in my truck, and told Barbara that I'd be home when the job sheets were complete. I took off at daylight on Monday. Going from small town to small town, which the Utah desert country has more than its share of, I knocked out a roof repair job, a couple of weedkilling assignments, and painted some markers, doors, and building trim.

I was profitably ahead of schedule when I got to Nephi, Utah. Their "community dial office" (small phone building) was a little different—a relay hut up on the side of the mountain. I drove up a snaking, dusty road and shuddered when I saw the height of the exhaust pipe from the diesel generator inside. I hated heights, but hated the thought of not being able to make payroll worse. So armed with a gallon of expensive 1500-degree resistant aluminum coating, I got up on the roof and then climbed the ladder on the stack and was soon doing my favorite thing: painting. In record time the stack was finished and gleaming wet. I was still up at the top, ready to descend, when I saw a small dark cloud moving toward me. I knew it wasn't a rain cloud, plus I could hear it hum.

Within seconds I was engulfed by a mass of flying gnats—it was like a horror movie. They didn't bite, just nearly suffocated me as they filled my eyes, ears, nose, and mouth. In thirty seconds it was over. The cloud of bugs was gone except for the 90 million or so of them that were stuck to the newly painted stack. My shining aluminum stack was now a black cylinder of tiny twitching wings. My first impulse was to sit down and bawl; my second was to go into the hut, start up the giant diesel engine, and burn those babies off. The third option was more rational and intelligent. The paint was good (very protective), and no one would ever see the stack up close, tall as it was and way up in the mountains as well. Starting up the motor and heating up the stack right now would probably be a bigtime fire hazard anyway. So I just left it and drove off to the next job. Almost forty years later now, I still have a strong urge to drive up there and see how many gnats are left.

I came home in four days—dirty, paint-covered, and unshaven—but having earned the $2000. Accomplishments like this went a long way toward building self-confidence and bank accounts.

The secret snackers

Don't point the finger without a solid amount of evidence in your fist. Rushing to judgment has been responsible for many a red face.

The most common injustice to the janitor is the accusation of thievery. When anything comes up missing in a building, the janitor is the first one questioned. I'm sure there are cases where janitors actually have been guilty, but as a rule they are an honest lot. They realize their vulnerability to suspicion. We also do all we can to select trustworthy people to begin with.

One "across the nation" call from a Bell System operation wanted to make me aware that the master pay station (phone booth) coin collecting key had been stolen and of course it had to be by one of the janitors. My people in that building were new and could barely identify a mop and a broom, so how, when, and where could they learn about this master key? I didn't know, but once one of our employees was suspected or accused we had to prove their innocence or dismiss them.

Proving innocence was rarely easy or clear cut when it came to thievery, but occasionally there was some satisfaction in seeing all suspicion dropped after an accusation. The management of a large Western Electric distribution center we cleaned complained continually about "our janitors" eating Bell System food. The evidence would be found strung throughout the building the next morning. Pieces of sandwiches would be found in halls or lounges, chicken bones right in the middle of the General Manager's rug, or half a wiener by the computer bank. Bell management would gather up the evidence and then chastise us stiffly for pilfering food and then discarding partly eaten morsels all over the building. Our people pleaded innocent of disturbing even a crumb of food. The phone company insisted it was our cleaning people and continued to complain whenever food fragments appeared.

It appeared that the verdict of guilty or innocent would never be officially read... until a Birmingham, Alabama operation many hundreds of miles away solved the problem and cleared Varsity's good name. They received an expensive piece of communications equipment from our building and upon opening the box, they discovered, nestled snugly in the packing material, six baby kittens. These little Bell orphans indicated at least two adult cats roaming freely in our building at night and hiding out in the daytime. It was their snacks that left the chicken bones and crusts distributed throughout the building. The Humane Society was called, and Varsity no longer had to take the rap.

My secondary service
as a heavenly visitor

Things occasionally are as they appear!

Charlie was a super salesman at our city's paint and glass store. My brothers and I, in our white uniforms, frequented the store almost as often as Charlie did the bottle. It was his good fortune to have a two-week vacation one winter and he chose the faraway wilderness town of Panguitch, Utah, to get away and relax.

Unbeknownst to Charlie, the Bell System had called me to bid a route of telephone buildings in that remote area, a bid I was awarded. So as fate would have it, I was there setting up the operation at exactly the same time Charlie was. I had no idea he was there, either.

At 1:05 one morning Charley was snuggled by a roaring fire at the local bar. It was minus thirty-two below outside; so cold a thick, icy fog had formed. Charlie was sipping a stiff drink (not his first of the evening), gazing out the window at the frosty mist. I was just finishing a floor stripping job at a small telephone office in that town, and had only one little job left before I could crash into my motel bed—servicing the phone booth outside the bar. I drove there, did a quick cleanup, and left.

A week later at home my brothers were chuckling over old Charlie's reformation—he had completely quit drinking! What was the cause of his turnabout? "You did it, Don," they roared, "You did it!"

Charlie's story to my brothers and other locals was a tale of mystic power, a vision striking enough to cause his conversion. "I was wide awake looking out the window when suddenly your brother's white truck appeared out of a cloud of ice and floated up to the window. I saw with my own eyes your brother leap out in a white suit, and then disappear into the fog." That hallucination did it—he quit drinking. My brothers strung him along through almost complete withdrawal, and then in a weak moment told him that I had actually been there. The jubilant, much-relieved Charlie regained his lost place at the bar quickly and I lost my first reformation client!

CHAPTER 5

WHOOPS!
(Employee Blunders)

Well... nobody's perfect!

Does your training program cover every part of the procedure—even the things you may take for granted that "everyone knows?"

YOU FIGURE it out—a bunch of eighteen-year-olds (mostly men in the early days of my business) who never even picked up a towel or a sock at home, go to work for a college cleaning company and the next day are in some huge house cleaning walls, windows, and carpeting with big machines, working around, under, and over beautiful drapes, furniture, grand pianos, collectibles, and china closets. Is everything going to go as planned?

Most things did but those that didn't involved some head-aches and heartaches, some replacement costs, some guilt, and often (no matter how disastrous the situation seemed at the time) some undeniable humor.

My journal over the years was full of minor disasters, devas-tating the day they happened, but survivable, and sometimes even somewhat beneficial in the end.

I'd send some employees on a supply or lunch errand across the street for the crew, and we'd never hear from them until the next day. They got lost; couldn't find their way back. Or they'd take the heat vent out of a floor to clean, and cover the hole with a canvas dropcloth, and our painter would set the leg of his ladder over it and climb up. Down he came, paint flying. Or they wouldn't tie big equipment onto the truck and it would fall out on the highway. They would lose keys, lose trucks, and lose equipment.

One new manager we hired, a big wheel, jetted in from many hundreds of miles away to attend our company meeting. In a building nearby, another company was having a meeting and he went to theirs, ate a big steak, and visited me the next morning. "Where were you?" we asked him. He thought he was at our meeting.

Once, six of us did a job in a nearby town, and when we were finished we loaded up, thanked the customer, and headed home in the crew truck. We were twenty miles away when someone said, "Where's Andy?" A quick count revealed that there were only five of us, so we returned. Andy was cleaning in a closet with the door closed, never even realizing we'd left. We'd been gone an hour and none of us could bring ourselves to tell him.

In Seattle we started a new contract that a new employee sold, telling the client (a bank) how good we were. The first night he used toilet bowl cleaner on fine wooden desks. Result: red faces and $25,000 worth of damage that we had to repair.

That same week one of our crews in Las Vegas mistakenly used bowl cleaner to clean some tarry tracks across the lobby of a fancy bank downtown. The acid reacted with the fiber of the carpeting and spread, turning each track into a huge

10" x 18" black burn of melted carpet. It looked as if Bigfoot had walked across the lobby to make a deposit. It ruined the carpet and we had to replace it, since we are insured for liability, not stupidity.

One promising young fellow we hired, trained briefly, then gave a key to the phone building office and told him to clean up the place. He must have mistaken "clean up" for "clean out," because on his second night he robbed the building and stole the telephone manager's car right out of the company lot.

In the 1980s we ran an expensive, but thorough safety program for the employees serving our new $500,000-a-month account cleaning a large department store. An hour after the session ended we had a "slip and fall" lawsuit there.

In the 1990s, one night in the parking lot of our newest big account, two of our pristine white Varsity trucks were wrecked. The only two vehicles in the lot, they ran into each other! A full list of employee blunders could fill this book.

Repairing, recovering from, or answering for your own mistakes (from low bids to bent fenders) is bad enough, but when it's your company and your crew, the buck and the blame always stops with the boss.

One day I was driving up from Ketchum to Sun Valley and noticed billows of smoke rolling up from the area of the shipping dock at the back of the lodge. I thought maybe some fireplace wasn't burning right; a closer view revealed that the entire dock was on fire; an even closer investigation revealed my janitor started it!

Our training hadn't covered the procedure for dealing with ashes and coals when cleaning a fireplace, and he had simply dumped the debris from his industrial vac into the paper-filled dumpster on the dock! Amazing how a powerful vacuum can resurrect a dead-looking coal. The few accidental fires I've been responsible for causing did little damage to structure but plenty to clients' confidence in me.

The operations manager said to me the next day, "Don, some of your people are dumber than six head of sheep!" I know how dumb one sheep is, so I got the message.

Free paint job

Another time, I asked one of our best workers if he could handle the large roof of the country club at a golf course. It had to be spray-painted red. He assured me he could cover every inch of it, that no job was too big or too small for him. He got the roof painted all right, and all of the cars parked around it (Saturday golfers). It cost an average of $400 each to clean and buff the cars afterward. The red paint came off the roof in a year, but we could hardly get it off the cars!

Curiosity kills a contract

Curiosity can kill more than contracts.

It took my cleaning company five years to finally get a shot at presenting a contract to the prestigious Bell Systems tower in downtown Los Angeles. My California manager and I were led into the CEO's office for an audience with him. Just then he got a call to the next room, so he politely seated us in his swank office, assuring us he would return momentarily.

In the room, in the middle of a conference desk, was a fancy phone system with lots of buttons. We couldn't help especially noticing one bright red button—one we'd never seen on a phone system before. The longer we sat, the more it intrigued us. We knew phones and phone buildings (having had contracts with over four hundred such offices in several states), but we'd never encountered anything just like this. Curiosity finally overcame my manager and he reached over and pushed the red button.

Sirens! It turned out to be the main fire alarm for that huge multi-story building. The whole building emptied immediately, as people scurried from their offices down stairways and into the streets. The CEO charged into his office ranting, as our appointed meeting time was replaced by the need to restore order to several hundred people. We never did get that contract, and I wasn't curious as to why.

The world's biggest hickey

No matter how experienced and professional we became, there were always new employees and personalities and the "X" or unknown factor.

In the mid-70s, at the end of a long day of carpet cleaning, our crews were putting away their tools. One young man had just taken the vacuum attachment from the end of a hose that was 200 feet long and two and a half inches in diameter. He was waiting for the operator to shut down the vacuum (powered by an 180-horse truck motor) it was attached to. The suction created by a motor like this is strong enough to lift a piano bench off the floor, and it fascinated the fellow. So instead of just holding the end of the hose, he began to experiment with it, as we might do with an impressive house vacuum, placing it playfully on his arm, his chest, his hand, etc.

But this was no house vacuum, as Bobby found out when he ran the hose by his face. It grabbed his chin, and uoomph! …there it stayed. He pulled and yelled and struggled like someone trying to ward off an attacking python in the jungle, but to no avail. The suction had firmly clasped his quivering chin. When the truck was finally shut down, the hose came loose. Bobby's troubles were far from over, however, for a giant round black and blue mark appeared circling his chin. He had a hard time explaining his circular tattoo for the next couple of weeks, but no trouble any more keeping the vacuum hose down on the floor where it belonged.

Dumpster diving adventures

Staying alert at trash time is a skill worth sharpening.

When something disappears into the trash, we always wonder, was it our fault, or the customer's? Or no one's fault at all? When something that shouldn't ends up in the dumpster, everyone panics. And no matter who put it there, guess who has to go digging for it. Us! In our fifty-plus years of cleaning, we've had some dramatic dumpster diving stories.

Varsity, for instance, lived by the Bell System policy that nothing extraneous should remain in the janitor closet. We proved this back in the fifties by throwing out seven boxes of long distance record cards which someone had stored in our closet, because no one in accounting knew where to store the new computer-generated calling cards. They were tossed late in the evening and hauled away by an efficient trash collector to the landfill early the next morning. By late afternoon that day (after the bills were buried under twenty feet of fill), the accounting department came to get their billing information for the month. But no cards were to be found. We were told that this dumpster dilemma ended up giving some AT&T customers the greatest long distance rate in history—the whole city got a month of free calls!

Two of our managers in Las Vegas realized one day that some important keys had been scooped off a desk and into the trash (medical trash, no less). It took them ten hours of digging through unmentionables to find the keys.

One of the supervisors in our Utah office, Robin Barnum, was informed one day that six sealed application envelopes were missing. A careful custodial audit revealed that a Varsity janitor, finding them in the trash, did chuck them in the dumpster. In the best trash-tragedy tradition, Robin rose to the cause and dove into the dump. But this was the 90s, and the degree of difficulty had increased. The problem was, the papers were in a giant trash compactor! This was no wimpy matter of sorting and rummaging as in earlier days. Oh no—Robin had to chisel apart and attempt to identify material squashed from thirty inches thick to three inches thick. His compactor expedition started as his fourteen-hour day finished at 9:30 P.M. By 3:30 A.M. (six hours of uncompacting later) the six flat envelopes appeared... slightly flatter. They were immediately given a quick Varsity cleaning and reinstated to their owner.

Efficiency that sucked

One change often makes another one necessary— watch for it!

We were awarded a contract once where the previous contractor had left the premises and equipment in sad shape. The client's vacuums were beat up, their bags overfilled, and the beater bar brushes on the bottoms worn to nubs. We repaired the 50-foot cords, emptied the bags, cleaned and shined the machines up, and ordered new beater brushes, all of the time making it clear to the client that we were the most efficient, fastest, and best janitor company on the planet.

By our contract's starting day the new brushes arrived and we installed them on those big, awkward old commercial upright vacuums. As the bristles on the old bars had worn down, the past cleaner had kept on lowering the bars closer to the carpet so what was left of the bristles could make contact with it. We snapped the new deep-bristle bars into the housings, not thinking about the height adjustment issue.

Our first night on the job, we wheeled a vacuum to the top of the hall that ran past the boss' glass-walled office, then plugged it in. The vacuum switch was left on by the previous user and the minute electricity reached the heavy-duty vac motor the new brush, now sunk deeply into the carpet and rotating forward, made the vacuum take off like a racecar. The operatorless machine was at full speed as it zipped past the boss' office. The sight of a totally self-running vacuum must have made him an instant believer that this new company was really as good as they claimed. When it crashed into the end of the hall, however, that glorious first impression faded fast.

Bank boo-boos

Some trash needs to be handled like treasure.

The lush, upscale, secure-feeling surroundings of banks did nothing to protect us from problems there.

Driving to the office one morning I noticed an unusual amount of litter on the road, and it got thicker as I got closer to the office. Easily identified as records of bank transactions, the trail was easy to follow and I was anxious to see what inept individual would be so careless. Then the paper trail turned down our street and onto our lot, and there was my Varsity pickup, the back loaded with open black garbage bags with a little remaining bank paper. We had a seven-day keep and destroy rule with bank trash, and my guy was hauling to destroy, but was much more efficient at distributing confidential documents all over town.

Another time, we contracted to clean a prominent bank in Reno. The manager was a high-strung fellow—even a misaligned paper punch could put him on edge—but he was fair. Our work there was a struggle. Reno was booming and even dishwashers and maids were getting $9.50 an hour. We had bid the building estimating labor costs at minimum wage ($2.15 at the time), so needless to say we had a hard time finding anyone worthwhile who was willing to work for that.

At first, the manager was nice and suggested we be a little more thorough and not miss a third of the wastebaskets. Next, he wrote notes that it would be much better if we locked the front door of the bank after we cleaned the entrance. He gradually moved to threats and demands, while we were hard put to even find a warm body to stick a cleaner's uniform on and send there. It was a nice bank and we needed the account to stay in Reno, so our manager would work there for three days and tune it up, and after he left it, would slide back to deplorable.

Finally the bank manager threatened cancellation. We begged and apologized and he yielded again. Then one day, driven to despair, he served us an official notice of cancellation of the contract. We couldn't blame him, but you wouldn't believe the sales job we did to keep it and he, against his better judgment, pardoned us yet again. We promised him that never again would anything go wrong.

The very next night we doubled the crew and spit-polished the building. However, on the second floor when the trasher collected the trash from the wastebaskets in one of those giant plastic bags, it was a long way down to the dumpster. Why go through all of those doors and halls, and all the way down the stairs, when he could just walk out on the second floor balcony and bingo, "bags away!" to the dumpster right in the alley below? This night his aim was bad and the bulging bags of confidential trash hit the edge of the bin and split apart. "Oh drat," said the janitor, "I'll have to go down and pick that up." Well, he forgot. That night a sudden squall of wind and rain came funneling up through the alley like a giant vacuum and at 7:30 the next morning when our favorite bank manager showed up, the door and front windows of the bank were plastered with dirty, rain-soaked overdraft notices and receipts and other private papers.

I'll never forget the bank manager's phone call. He was so mad he couldn't even talk—he just sputtered and snorted, trying to catch his breath and say something bad enough for the occasion. At the end of his mad murmurings and ravings, however, we did hear plainly "You're fired!" Many years later now, I still feel that once we got our act together in Reno we should have cleaned his bank free for a month.

At the banks we cleaned not all goofs were ours. In one branch bank, the manager was carrying a full day's transactions (deposits, checks, etc.) downstairs for processing in a big Rubbermaid trash tub he'd borrowed from a janitor closet. He stopped by the restroom on the way, and set the tub on a drinking fountain while he was inside. Our janitor, walking by, saw the beat-up looking tub (which we used to gather trash), picked it up, and fed the contents into a very efficient shredder. By the time they figured out what had happened there was only one

alternative: hire a small army of college students to tape and glue all of those thousands of shreds back together.

Condo conundrum

Cleaners are often called to places with no convenient lunchroom or other facilities, so plan ahead.

Mark Browning was unequalled, except maybe by Arlo, for colorful and eventful experiences in the company and was constantly in situations that never happened before and would probably never happen again. A classic was the day our paint crew was about finished with a large condominium project. The units were new and hadn't been sold and dozens of craftspeople were still running around finishing things up. There were no plumbing hookups yet and as nature would have it, Mark needed a restroom. Since there were none to be had, he picked up an empty gallon paint can and walked to the finished but unoccupied condo next door to take a rest stop. To be discreet he went upstairs and chose the closet of the master bedroom for the event. He had finished and was opening the door to leave when he heard a loudspeaker outside: "Now, ladies and gentlemen, we'd like to present for your pleasure and inspection the latest in all-electric interiors. The tour will begin here at the front door."

Mark froze in his tracks, as he heard the tromp of dozens of potential customers gathered for this grand opening tour. Beads of sweat emerged on his forehead as he tried to think of a way out with his partially filled paint can, but he was upstairs and there was no gracious escape. The crowd was coming up the stairs now and the guide was saying, "...and just wait until you see the elegant master bedroom with its spacious modern closets." Browning grasped the doors and braced himself solidly against them, so when the tour guide attempted to open the door he couldn't. It was quite a tug of war but only lasted a few minutes as the tour guide tugged and heaved to pull the door open. Mark, his very honor and dignity at stake, had a death grip on the inside and wouldn't give an inch. The tour guide finally gave up and left, muttering something about calling the carpenter to examine it.

We became experts at bidding and estimating jobs, but all of us err and even Mark was no exception. The manager of the Sun Valley Company in charge of Mt. Baldy needed a reinforced concrete storage cache for dynamite built on the side of the mountain, near where they most frequently blasted to prevent snow slides from developing into avalanches. Mark looked the situation over and, being quite a builder, figured up a bid for it. When the time came to figure the cost of the concrete, plus hauling it up the side of the mountain, he decided he'd better get an exact figure. The going price for concrete delivered on the valley floor by the Redi-Mix people was $21 a cubic yard. When Mark asked a contractor, who was mixing concrete on the side of the mountain, how much it cost to have it delivered up on the mountain, the man asked him how much he would need. "I figure about ten yards," Mark answered. "Well," the man said, "let's figure about $200."

Mark was surprised at the reasonable cost, secured the contract easily, and constructed the cache. All was well until the bill for the concrete arrived—it was over $4000! The cost quoted was per yard, not for the whole amount! Mark had made some good profits that summer and had a nice commission coming. Needless to say, he was a sick young businessman as he sat for hours that evening at his desk, shaking his head and wondering how he could come out on a job that he bid for $2500 when he had $4800 worth of material costs.

Quickie decluttering

Some of my fellow pros in Chicago, up on the 20th floor of a big office building, were demonstrating how the new swing-in windows operated, and each opened a window on his side of the room. Must have caught an all-time perfect wind direction. It was like opening an airplane window at 30,000 feet. It sucked all the loose paper out of the office in four seconds.

Let the janitors do it!

It is truly amazing how we all behave, even we professional cleaners, when we know there is someone cleaning up for or behind us. My company cleaned one of the recreation lounges at a major university and would often be frustrated at all the popcorn left all over the place after its daily or nightly use. One evening we (our cleaning company and the university janitors) rented it and had a party. And when we were ready to leave, popcorn was strung all over the place, just like usual, and one of our people said, "Just leave it, the custodians will get it," forgetting that... we *were* the custodians!

CHAPTER **6**

Never a Dull Moment: In Homes or at the Office

EVERY PROFESSION has its high points, but few equal the life of a janitor. Not a week goes by that isn't loaded with memorable experiences. There is rarely a situation that you can't learn a great lesson from and have a barrel of fun doing it.

Humor, color, and good times were a constant reward to compensate for some of the struggles of providing toilet-cleaning services to the public. Because our accounts ranged from a quiet little house in the village to a millionaire's mansion, schools to theaters and stadiums, offices, factories, and hundreds of other operations, our exposure to life was more than fascinating.

Because society as a whole seems to believe we are so unimportant, we cleaners are almost invisible, they allow us everywhere, at any hour. We have the keys and authority to enter even the most sensitive areas of people's lives and properties, so we see and hear everything. The adventure that most people hunt and pay for, we get right on the job, constantly.

The world's biggest ashtray

Cleaning jobs can include some unbelievable extremes, requiring tolerance, a sense of humor and challenge, and often just plain endurance.

One Western truck terminal we cleaned was a wild one. The truckers would stomp in wearing their heavy boots, missing the 30-foot heavy-duty, grease and mud catching mat, cross the floor, and grab their orders. Upon reading them, the drivers would often throw them on the floor and jump up and down on them, dislodging cleatsful of boot debris on not just the documents, but our newly cleaned floors. They'd roll out a string of censored phrases, and yell something like, "A double trailer of potato chips across those windy Wyoming flats? No way—I won't go. Old Joe took a single of paper towels there and the blankety blank wind just about blew him over the cliff. Are you trying to kill me? @!(*&##+)@%&!!" Then the trucker would do another dance on the orders and pick them up and lay them on a clean, freshly polished desk.

We called this particular account the world's biggest ashtray. We would set out twelve or fourteen ashtrays and when we arrived the next day to clean there would be three butts in one tray and 478 crushed cigarettes on the floor, creating a striking pattern of crisscross burns. Most of the ashtrays would be gone, taken by the truckers for their sleeper cabs. We tried screwing, nailing, and gluing them down, buying bigger ones, ugly ones, etc., but it didn't faze the truckers. They continued to remove them and throw their butts on the floor.

The lunchroom resembled a feedlot corral, only dirtier. Someone would eat his lunch on the corner of a table, leaving it covered with half-filled pop cans, a few crusts, and some olive pits or apple cores. The next trucker, finding no room because of the previous snackers' mess, would pick a place he wanted and then like a giant grizzly, with a grunt and swipe of the arm, scrape the whole mess onto the floor, polish a spot clean with his sleeve, and proceed to eat. After eating he would leave the remains of his lunch and the next trucker would follow the same place-selection routine.

We used snow shovels to gather the debris and scoop it up into the two 55-gallon trash barrels that were always in the room (and always empty). The world's biggest ashtray and the lunchroom were hard to clean, but the restroom was even worse. Once inside the door, mother nature's call was answered, but not necessarily in the fixtures provided for the purpose. Jamie Warnock, the state manager and sometimes the janitor there, felt the solution might be hanging some signs that played off the truckers' heroes. "Marty Robbins doesn't pee on the floor," "Burl Ives doesn't throw his butts in the urinal," "Raquel Welch wonders if you do these things in your own home."

Truckers are a great bunch of guys, so excuse the janitor's eye view.

Green clean

Doing the job the customer's way—even when you know better—is sometimes part of the job.

We were doing construction cleanup prior to the tenants moving into a three million square foot building in Atlanta. One work order was to scrub down the newly installed tile in the kitchen. The kitchen was huge, and you might imagine the size of the appliances needed to service the employees in a building this big. The building's maintenance manager had emphatically specified the exact cleaner to be used on this special tile floor with its special grout—some imported acid product. So we obeyed.

From the beginning it didn't feel right, and we should have questioned the big wheel, but we didn't. The fumes from the acid had some strange chemical reaction with all of the stainless steel fixtures, and by the time the floor was done, all of the beautiful stainless steel appliances and accessories had turned green—terrible vomit green. We were sick about it, but fortunately not liable for the result. We were sure glad we didn't pick the cleaner. We never thought about what it might have done to our lungs.

Vegas adventures

In Vegas we seemed to have more interest and motivation across the board. On one trip there, a very quiet and shy gentleman, Bob Garcia, a family man who would never think of uttering a profane phrase, put his head down in great embarrassment when I asked him how it was going. "Boy, you won't believe what happened," he said.

"I was going up to clean the Charleston building, and when I stopped at a stop sign, a white Corvette convertible pulled up right next to me. Sitting in this car was a young lady with (as far as you could see) nothing on. She was topless, and I tried not to stare, but then another car pulled up alongside that one in the third lane. This was a white Corvette too and the young woman driving it didn't appear to be fully dressed either. When they spotted each other they both stood up in their seats at the red light and started shaking and dancing, and both of them were completely minus any apparel at all. I couldn't believe it," he said. "You know I come from Wyoming and we have horses that run alongside of you sometimes, but this was unreal."

I noticed later, though, that production in that building went up about 50 percent that night. I don't know whether it was the urge to get home as quickly as possible, or to drive up and down the strip a few more times to check out any further body-shaking competitions.

In the 70s one of our prestigious accounts in Las Vegas was a bank chain consisting of a large downtown skyriser and several branch banks scattered throughout the city. In one of these coffee spills were a constant problem. Coffee with cream and sugar in it is difficult to remove if it is not cleaned up immediately. So our custodian there did an enterprising bit of work. Unable to please the branch manager with his ability to remove coffee spots, he came up with the ingenious idea of saving all of the leftover coffee from breaks and the lunchroom for a couple of weeks. Then one night instead of shampooing the carpet with the specified coconut-oil, high foaming shampoo, he filled the tank of the machine with coffee and cleaned the whole carpet with it, staining it all the same color as the spills. The place smelled like the grand opening of a new Starbucks for a few weeks, but the carpet looked great.

> *Creative camouflage is sometimes the last tool*
> *in the box.*

Our office in Vegas was broken into three times, the door beaten down with a crowbar, and our company checks stolen plus some cash. Right after the second break-in, our manager ran to the bank and told the teller not to honor any yellow Varsity checks. "Like this one?" she chirped, holding up a check she'd just cashed. "Where'd you get that?" our manager questioned. The teller leaned over and whispered, "From the guy right behind you writing another one!" The thief with our whole pad of checks was indeed five feet away—a silent call for the cops and he was jailed.

I got a hushed call another day telling me most of my good accounts were from the Mafia, great news! Do a poor job and get a cement mop bucket.

Remember, janitors work at night, and Vegas is alive at night. When my employees weren't stopping robberies, being flashed, solicited by prostitutes or unions, getting beat up, or their trucks vandalized, they cleaned buildings.

I wondered at times if we were just plain incompatible with Vegas—it seemed that even our best accounts here would end up in trouble. We had a nice contract to clean the Sultan Spa (name changed to protect the undressed), an exclusive women's health club. Once inside the spa, clothes were replaced by skimpy, clingy leotards or nothing. Because everyone somehow thinks janitors are dumb, or sexless, no one made any effort to conceal herself and just flaunted and flopped at will. It didn't seem to bother the ladies to zip and bounce around in the nearly nude, but it sure cut cleaning production down. Needless to say, for our young men, this became a much sought after place to work, especially the carpeted area near the lockers and pool, which was getting worn from over-vacuuming. Then, too, prospective new accounts always liked to see some of your present accounts (to check out the quality of your work), and knowing we had the Sultan, you can guess where all of our potential new customers wanted to go. The Sultan and its clientele didn't appreciate periodic parades of goggle-eyed building managers.

Shaping up here followed a carefully laid out schedule. Monday was showgirl night (chorus line beauties from the Vegas stages), Tuesday senior citizen night, and Thursday we tabbed plus size night. Everyone fought for Monday, and Tuesday nighters suffered depression. As for plus size night, it almost caused us to finally let the contract go. An employee working that night was mopping the locker room when a 425-pound hunk of woman skipped out of the shower. My employee threatened to sue for loss of any and all sex drive! There were so many arguments over scheduling, we were relieved when the spa management decided to do the cleaning themselves.

In case anyone wondered, yes,
janitors are human, too.

Gator aid

One time several building managers got to swapping stories about how fast their custodians could carry trash from the building and dump it in the outside bins. The L.A. man told a story about a thug with a knife prowling around outside, so his custodian moved fast and carried a gun when he dumped the trash. A Northern manager bragged on how cold it was where he came from (forty below), so his man dumped it fast, or froze. Another manager told how his janitor dumped it from the top of the building—everyone trying to top the last story.

Finally an old Southern Bell manager, gesturing toward the chain-link fence marking the boundary between his building and the Florida swamps behind it, said, "Tell you what, men. See that little hole under that fence there?" We all looked and saw an eighteen-inch tunnel under the fence. "Well about trash time, an alligator comes out and under that fence, and you ought to see my janitor dump the trash!"

One day we got a call from a woman who wanted a bid on cleaning the walls and ceiling of her living room and kitchen. When we got there, there was a plank set between two stepladders, at a height of only about five feet. The woman said her husband had intended to do the job, but when he got up on the plank he got a sudden attack of height-a-phobia and ended up lying down on the plank clutching it with a death grip. His wife couldn't talk or pry him off of it, so she had to call the fire department to come rescue him.

Needless to say, we got the job.

Family ingenuity

A fresh look—and strong enough desire—will often find a way.

Stories about our children could fill any book, and without question they teach more lessons of life than any school even dreams about. My youngest son, Rell, came to me one day in his senior year of high school and said, "Dad, remember when you said that someday you were going to do two things: grow a beard and buy a Porsche?" (I was known for my conservatism and would never do either.) "Well, Dad, we won't hold you to the beard but there is a Porsche in the paper and it's a good deal." I interrupted, "No way, Rell!"

Well I didn't promise, but I did make the statement, so I tried to figure a way out of it to satisfy all at hand. Then it came, the perfect out—a deadbeat who owed me money and would never pay in two millenia. I handed the bill to Rell and said, "Here, collect this and you can use it to buy the car." No chance!

Barbara and I left for two weeks in Hawaii the next morning. Thirty minutes after we arrived there, the phone rang. It was my CFO, who asked, "How do you want to insure this Porsche?" Never underestimate a kid's ability when they want something!

I was of course shocked but also intrigued by the question of how he had accomplished this seemingly impossible feat of collection. I asked him how he got the money so fast—all of it, no less. "I went to see his mother," he said. Kids know mothers, all right!

When my little mail order cleaning supply business started doing several hundred dollars worth of business a day (and supplies were selling well at all of my seminars, too), it was plain to see that spray bottles were a strong seller. We were ordering a few cases at a time and moving them quickly. My idea of getting white opaque bottles with "Life After Housework" (harkening to the title of my first bestseller) printed on them called for a minimum 5,000-bottle order. My office people and mail order manager gasped at this staggering figure; almost beyond comprehension. Then the salesman said you got a real price break on a 10,000-unit order, and that interested me. Where was the really big price break?" I asked. "30,000," he said. At that quantity printed bottles were only 17 cents apiece—what a deal! And eventually we would sell them. My staff held their breath. "He wouldn't!" they said. But I did. With total faith in an up and coming business, I went for it and ordered 30,000 customized spray bottles, figuring that having this many would push us to sell them.

But I hadn't thought through the logistics of this. I knew the order was only about $5000, not bad for an eternal supply of personalized bottles, but when they came, the freight bill was an unprecedented $2300. Then I walked outside to see the truck they came in. Each box contained 100 bottles, and the boxes were huge things, about three feet high and two feet wide, and the 53-foot long trailer on the truck was jammed with them. There was even one in the empty seat beside the driver. We had to fill the shop, the garage, part of my office, the rug cleaning truck garage, and some of the sidewalk outside to get the truck unloaded. Then I drove many pickup loads home and for months our living room and garage were stacked high with boxes. Those spray bottles were like locusts for three years afterward. With us moving them out at the rate of 15 bottles a day we had a five-year supply. Then opaque went out of style because you couldn't see the color of the cleaning solution inside, and I wore out the boxes moving those babies around.

Our spray bottle backlog led to all kinds of excitement, including a call from the principal of the high school one day. "Don, we've had a water gun episode that has affected the entire school. Your son furnished high-power spray bottles for the entire student body!" Of course I intended to make an innocent plea and asked what made him suspect me, Mr. Clean. "Because," he said, "all of the bottles have 'Don Aslett Life After Housework' printed on them."

Cornering my son Rell, I got his justification. "Well, Dad, you taught us to be enterprising. I knew you had plenty so I put adjustable nozzles on them, loaded my car and truck full of them, and sold them for $1 each. They outshot the ordinary water guns unbelievably and think of the good advertisement."

I guess he might have had a point there. I eventually offered them free as giveaways. People were slow to take them, even free—they figured anyone dumb enough to have a thousand spray bottles in his living room must have a con scheme going.

When considering economies of scale, don't forget about obsolescence.

The rug rap

When cleaning, it's important to know where all the members of the family are—even the four-legged and furry ones.

We were finishing painting touchup on a new modular home, and part of the family was there trying to move in. A couple of other contractors were there, too, attending to final details, including a flooring crew applying some carpetlike floor covering in a dining area. The material came in large rolls, which were swiftly kicked to unroll them across the room. Apparently (as we could hear from the next room), after the floor covering was rolled out, there was a lump under it. One installer said to the other, "Harry, you idiot, did you leave your glove under this?"

"No, Mike   both gloves are in my pocket."

"Well then it must be glue or an air bubble; gimme that two-by-four stud block."

He laid the block of wood over the little hump and beat it flat with a 20-ounce hammer. About then, a little boy wandered to the edge of the room and asked, "Mister, have you seen my hamster?"

I've heard this story in other versions, but I am certain it really happened at least once, to us, with a house full of witnesses and a hamsterless kid!

Un-dulling routine work

One supervisor delighted in confusing and challenging the maids who cleaned the public ladies' room on the main level of the famous Sun Valley Lodge. He would sneak into a stall, set a pair of men's shoes in front of the stool, and then drape the legs of an empty, old pair of trousers from the seat down onto the shoes, which from outside the stall created the illusion of a male intruder. It caused much screaming, embarrassment, and decision-making as to just who of the ladies had to go tell the imaginary male that the pause that refreshes was not to be taken in this particular room. (How the supervisor managed to lock the door after he left the stall was never revealed.)

Some Raleigh Bell janitors did the reverse, placed an inflatable rubber female form on the stool in the men's restroom. The evening janitor was so surprised when he opened the door that he leaped back, striking his head on the stall support and knocking himself unconscious. He was found lying next to the harmless latex lass—try explaining that to the fellow workers who found you.

Another time, part of one of the men's restrooms in the Salt Lake City airport was roped off with a sign that said, "This section closed to conserve water." Some man scrawled on the edge of the sign, "I came to make a deposit, not a withdrawal."

It seemed there was always a hitch to even the best idea. Someone invented a magnetic metal strip that could be mounted on the front of an upright vacuum, to pick up paper clips, screws, and other metal objects before they got sucked in and damaged the vacuum. It increased the weight of the vac, but worked well enough. But every time I got near a metal wastebasket, it suddenly became a new addition to the vacuum.

The most mundane things can appeal to some thieves—even items that have "hard work" implicit in them.

On a job site once, one of our subcontractor's workers tried to steal one of our expensive 100-foot extension cords. He was caught when someone who knew him asked when he put on all the weight. He had taken off a loose pair of coveralls and wrapped the cord like a mummy wrapping around his body, from his lower hips to his armpits, then put the coveralls back on, and tried to waddle off the job.

Who would want what a janitor has? Yet we often have things stolen out of our janitor closets—people take things and carry them home, or leave them somewhere else when they are done with them. Someone stole one of our rug extractor trailers in Phoenix once, and we found it ourselves, inside a big fence. We told the police and they said, "Good, let's leave it there a few days and see if we can use it to trap and catch the thief." We agreed, but never got it back, because someone else stole it from the first thief.

Pass the pop bottle

*Why do we sometimes spend more time dodging
a job, than doing it would ever take??*

I was bidding the cleaning of a suburban office complex in Las Vegas, and on my first visit there I noticed a flattened, worn, but still recognizable empty Sprite pop can on the lawn on my way into the building. I also noticed the grounds person (landscaping contractor) arriving and working during my visit. When I left I noticed the can was now in the parking lot.

The next day, when I came back, I noticed the can on the sidewalk by the entrance to the building—the parking lot maintenance person had undoubtedly chucked it off his territory onto the building cleaner's turf. So when I came back out, having signed a contract now to be the building cleaner, I kicked it back onto the lawn where it was originally.

Two days later, their gardener came again, and afterward I noticed the can was back in the parking lot, and true to routine a couple of days later when we showed up to clean there it was on the sidewalk again; our area. Too irritated to just pick it up and dispose of it, we kicked it back onto the lawn again, the lazy landscape contractor's territory.

This battle of whose trash it was went on for weeks, all of us bent on seeing if the other guy would yield. Now you know why the can was worn and flat. It's been twenty years since that contract and every time I pass through Vegas I have an urge to veer off my route and go see if the can is still rotating between three vengeful contractors. How would you bet?

The bird house

One of the homes our crew cleaned was nicknamed the "bird house." In the center of the living room the owner, a bird lover, had built a deluxe roost for his six-pound parrot out of plastic pipe and fittings. The bird flew through the house at will, and it even had its own private bedroom. Its cage was the whole house, the walls and floor, its litter box. They were all streaked and peppered with parrot poop. The drapes were just hanging strips and shreds from the bird's talons clinging to and clawing them.

Top dog

At one home the owner's favorite dog was a pest and always sniffed out and ate the crew's lunch. When the owner returned home one day she found her dog up on the roof. I had no idea how it got there or who did it, but I did notice some smug faces while I was trying to explain to the owner that the dog probably jumped up there chasing a bird.

Dusting drama

Most of us in the cleaning industry are quick to "one up" the cleaning adventures of others, and may even exaggerate a bit any unique or bizarre event that crops up in our regular routine. Conversing once with a Southern Bell telephone supervisor, I had just related what I thought was an unbeatable "item found while dusting" story, and he said, "Follow me." (We were inspecting a small telephone equipment building near a swampy area in Florida.) He walked up to a high electrical panel box, which he proceeded to swipe with a dustcloth, picking up (knocking off) a dead frog. Another rigor mortised, barely identifiable object on top of some nearby equipment he identified as the remains of a "walking catfish." How or why it got into the building and up off the floor stumped me, and I had to admit it took top place in weird dusting finds.

Cat capers

Cleaning today often encompasses critters—those you must clean around, and those that require removal or relocation.

Fifty years of cleaning around cats sure took lots of imagination and energy.

I always took jobs and customers seriously and didn't have to lighten up much because I always had some quick-witted, bold guys on the crew who took care of that.

One woman (who had a very nice home) also had a pure white longhaired cat, rhinestone collar and all. She was very impressed by the job Mark Browning did painting the inside of her cupboards, and Browning with a pretty convincing straight face, explained that he'd dipped the cat in a roller pan of paint, then tossed it in each cupboard, closed the door, and beat on the door. The frightened cat distributed the paint perfectly, he claimed. (Knowing Browning, I couldn't help wondering if he'd actually tried it.)

Another time, I was on a cleaning job miles from home and was about finished, when I found the woman's cat stretched out on the last big couch I had been hired to shampoo. That stubborn critter just wouldn't "shoo," and the owner finally leaped in front of me and my big upholstery extractor.

"Oh no, Don, Pixie has ashotoxic nodularity, and can't be alarmed in any way." So she offered to pay me for not cleaning the couch.

While in New York in 1985 meeting with the NY Port Authority manager then in charge of the 115-story World Trade Center buildings, we were discussing "unique building maintenance problems." Their most recent being cats—huge wild cats inside this high-class office complex. How could it be? Seems that as the structure was being erected, many of the city's stray cats discovered that if they hung around the construction site, the hundreds of workers would share scraps from their lunches. So for two or three years, as the building came together, not only did a cat colony grow comfortable there, but also fat and healthy. Until the last few weeks of completion the building remained open, so cats were able to go inside as the finish work progressed.

Result? When the building was complete, many experienced, untamed "phantom of the opera" cats were sealed inside. They hid in false ceilings, hollow wall spaces, crawlspaces, and the like, roaming and eating where they could. During one big executive meeting in the new and now fully occupied building, suddenly an acoustic ceiling tile collapsed and a huge cat came flailing down and landed on the conference table, going berserk before the surprised attendees. Containing the dust-covered cat proved a bigger problem than was at hand in the business agenda, because it was big, wild, and terrified!

We did bid on maintaining the World Trade Center, and our disappointment at not securing the contract was lessened when we learned that the contractor who did lost 124 new vacuums the first night (they were stolen!).

Fair favors

Any top-notch cleaning or maintenance person does a few freebies for worthy causes to flex his skills and help spread the gospel of clean.

Everyone in our community knew that a pro cleaner, painter, and construction man had equipment around. A bonanza for borrowers! After years of using my stuff, it was discovered that things were even better if I accompanied it, so they borrowed me too. Thus I enjoyed a lifetime of donating, and two such episodes I remember well.

It seems that several of the fairground buildings in Downey, Idaho, had looked shabby for years. Ernie Garrett was an energetic community advocate and a friend of mine (and that year he was head of the fair board). So he logically thought, why try to organize the whole community to deal with this when I have Don Aslett and his equipment?

He called. "Don, I have a little painting job down here and ten cans of paint."

"Sure, Ern, I have a half day on Tuesday and I'll bring my airless sprayer."

When I got there the cans of paint were five gallons each, and there were four stadium-sized barns to paint. I gasped, and Ernie the optimist said, "We have to get it done because the fair opens in two days!"

"You mix, stir, strain, and keep the tank of the airless filled with paint, and I'll go for it," I replied.

The buildings were big, but all low with open fronts, and needed no trimming or dropcloths, just a few light fixtures shielded. An airless is a paint sprayer that doesn't use air—it puts the paint under pressure with a hydraulic pump. This "gun," run by electricity, puts out a three-foot blast of paint, and when the going is unobstructed it can drain a five-gallon can of paint faster than a kid can slurp down a McDonald's milkshake with a big straw. Since there was little preparation needed, no wind to drift the spray around, and three appreciative members of the fair board watching in awe, Ern and I painted all four of those buildings white in five hours. He, a 380-pound giant, was panting and the hydraulics were hot when I got done, but it was a feat never repeated, not even by a whole crew.

The rodeo board in my hometown of McCammon heard of this painting miracle to the south and the head of the town committee, Tom (also a friend) called. "Don, we need badly to have the stadium bleachers painted and I have the paint." "Sure" was the only choice I really had. He also promised a crew of men (local "cowboys," to be exact) to help push around and feed the machine. My wife Barbara, eight months pregnant with our youngest son, came with me and my pickup load of equipment. Tom was a nice guy, but a bargain hunter, and the paint he had was 1942 Army surplus, battleship deck grit safety yellow. It seemed to consist of 1/3 sand, 1/3 solvent, 1/3 toxic fumes, and eye-blinding yellow pigment. It had jelled to the consistency of pudding from sitting around in storage so long, I realized, as I pondered the fact that the tip on my spray gun cost $200 (like $500 today). The miracle of converting it to a liquid again was comparable to raising the dead, and guess who performed it?

When it came to real work those "cowboys" were about worthless, and to entice them into the spirit of volunteerism Tom had bought a few cases of beer. They drank and Barbara and I worked. When that bright yellow paint began to cover those old, beat-up seats, there were cheers and rejoicing and even more drinking. Soon we had a bleacher full of drunks, and lugging buckets and the machine across the area was Barbara. Not one community cowboy came to the rescue. The job was a topic at local bars for years among the cowboys, who still think they did it.

Passing through our Cleaning Center store one day, I noticed a customer studying the label on some rather strong bowl cleaning acid. He said his toilet was plugged up, and wondered if this stuff would dissolve it. "Do you have any idea what's in there?" I asked.

"A bikini," he said.

"Really? How did it get in the toilet?" I replied.

"One of the kids threw it in," he answered.

Well, I had never tried to dissolve a bikini in a toilet drain before. I doubted that the acid would break down the synthetic it was probably made of (at least not quickly), so suggested that he try fishing it out with a hook. I also told him that for this particular purpose good old Drano caustic cleaner would probably work better than the acid.

"I've tried that before and it didn't work," he said.

"Really? Well how many times has this happened?"

"Well, it's happened a couple times before."

"What did you do?"

"We finally flushed it down."

"Aren't you running out of bikinis?" I asked.

"Oh no, no!" he said. "Zucchini, not bikini in there!!"

I knew then what he should use and was relieved that his better half still had a little something to wear on her southern half.

And speaking of scanty panties, they end up in stranger places than toilets. One of my vacuum repair buddies told me once that a husband and wife brought back a new vacuum they had just bought, because it wasn't working—seemed to have no suction. The "take-charge" husband had a lot of complaints about the vacuum (and his wife as well) as the repairman removed the vacuum housing, but had little to say when the repairman pulled out a bikini bottom that had been wrapped around the fan... a fetching little number that his wife had never seen before!

Discretion is the word when the janitor uncovers incriminating evidence!

CHAPTER 7

The Janitor's Nemesis:
Complaints

Pleasing some of the people some of the time

BEING IN a profession where every client considers himself an expert on cleaning and where people always take the positive for granted and report only the negative, we weren't unfamiliar with complaints.

If there is one strong personal trait a person needs to be a janitor, it is the ability to take criticism and listen to complaints. Janitors, like anyone else, do need to correct their errors, but they unquestionably get much more negative feedback than they deserve. It is natural for us to seek a scapegoat and the janitor is nailed for a vast number of problems that he or she had nothing to do with. If a tree blows down across the road from the building, the janitor is at fault for watering it too much and weakening the roots, or for not watering it enough.

Some clients (did they have unhappy lives at home??) seemed to make a profession of picking on the janitors. We deserved some reminding for oversights and got it, generally in the form of notes left pinned to the cleaning closet door or stuck to a buffer handle. This was usually less brutal then being dressed down in person. The more chicken and creative clients were seasoned trap setters (see page 142). I saved a few of the more memorable ones.

You wouldn't believe the complaints you get when you're in charge of the cleaning. The complaints never ceased, no matter how perfectly you trained the janitor or even if he was a local professor working part time. One building occupant broke his leg while flushing the toilet. Another complaint I had to work out on a busy day was one from a department store owner who said my painters working in the street display window had left (on purpose, he claimed) the mannequins in all sorts of erotic positions when they moved them, and a crowd was forming on the street. How about this one: "Aslett, your floors in here are too shiny. The reflection allows people to see up the ladies' dresses." Another client saw our hungry student cleaner retrieving perfectly good food out of a wastebasket and eating it and complained violently about us eating their food.

Once we were accused of stealing belts off some of the clothing racks in a department store we cleaned. All of the workers pleaded innocent. The culprit was finally caught. On our 36" wide-space vacuum there were six belts wrapped around the giant brush roll. When the vacuum was pushed back under a slack or trouser rack, any belt end touching or near the floor was sucked off the garment. The buckle probably clicked a bit as it went in, but the janitor, lost in a world of earphone music, didn't hear it.

On one building we cleaned we were told, "The customer is unhappy—too many complaints." So we went all-out to please them, and no more complaints. Then they called us in and said, "There aren't enough complaints, so we must be paying you too much."

When I first started cleaning, it didn't take long for me to discover this complaint business. When I washed a woman's greasy kitchen down, she didn't toss confetti on me as I went out the door or send roses to thank me the following day. She was more likely to vault to the attic the moment you left, get out her expired husband's old magnifying glass, and go over every inch of wall and woodwork you had just cleaned. Most women believed that no one (especially a man) could possibly clean fast and well. Things like this often followed.

The shadow of doubt

Yield graciously to unhappy customers—in any business you will get a few.

I was home one day catching up on studying for my college classes when the phone rang. It was Mrs. Greasewall. "Mr. Aslett, there's a streak on my ceiling." I groaned but realized my reputation needed to be as spotless as my work. So I dressed, cranked up the old Varsity truck, and drove across town to her home (my bill for this job had been all of $9).

"See, see, see!" she said, grabbing me by the arm and pulling me down to her 5'2" eye level. "That big black streak!" I could indeed discern a mark there and went out to the truck and got all of my gear, cranked up the wall machine, and re-cleaned the spot. But the mark wouldn't budge. I was sure I'd done a good job the first time, but now, no matter how hard I cleaned this ceiling I couldn't get the streak out. By now she was whimpering and almost shouting, "It wasn't there before you came. I paid good money to get a good job." I had some great answers for her, but kept them confined to thoughts.

I worked and worked on it and would probably have been there all night (as she wore a hole in the floor pacing and raving louder with each round). Suddenly in one of her wild gestures she hit the pole lamp and the black streak on the ceiling darted in perfect rhythm with the swing of the lamp. It was a shadow all the time! She was more obnoxious apologizing than she was complaining and I went home, passing my first test of public relations—but by no means my last.

The case of the cut carpet

Many a dispute would be dissolved by taking a minute to look at the facts.

New little cleaning companies like ours, especially back in the late 50s, were babes in the wood from a legal standpoint. We knew little about liabilities, less about licenses and labor laws, and few bureaucrats had taken serious heed of a few struggling college kids working part time.

Then came a letter from an attorney, representing a client who claimed our machine had cut slits in their carpet. Facing our first lawsuit, we were of course much alarmed, so we secured an attorney and huddled with him. Making a long (like most stupid legal hassles) story short, we (both lawyers and both parties) eventually met in a courtroom to battle it out.

The husband and wife suing us could have stepped right out of the *Beverly Hillbillies*, and most of their furnishings if given to Salvation Army would have been rejected. They had a picture of their thirty or forty-year-old carpet (which had surely never been cleaned before) with indeed long slits in it, which they claimed had been made by our machine. We hadn't touched or cleaned the carpet, only washed the walls, so the judge asked us to produce our wall machine, a twenty-pound suitcase-sized box with large soft rubber casters on the bottom. "That's the machine!" the plaintiff yelled.

After examining it, neither the judge, our attorney, nor their attorney could see how it could possibly cut a tough carpet and the slits (all over the place, even under the couch) turned out to be seam separations from age and wear. Case dismissed—we were cleared; had won. Won what? The minute the judge smacked his gavel the two attorneys jumped over the court railing, shook hands, and went off to lunch arm in arm, while we the sued and the suers sat on opposite sides of the now quiet courtroom blinking at each other, both several hundred dollars poorer over a small carpet that could have been replaced with new for about $80. Welcome to the American legal system! Our legal experiences only went downhill from there.

Some complaints had their compensations. A new, young, cocksure manager just given authority over a number of small rural telephone offices we cleaned took great delight in needling us over any slight cleaning misdeed, telling us each time, "I'm paid to be a hardass!" One day he told us that there was a disaster at the Lewisville CDO (community dial office) and to follow him out there. We pulled in behind his company truck and followed. He seemed to be taking a new and longer route there, and finally Arlo nudged me and said, "Don, he's lost—he can't find the office!" And sure enough, he couldn't. He drove up and down and down and around and over hills and rural roads late into the afternoon, hunting desperately for it and

Arlo and I stayed right behind him. The longer he hunted the more stubborn he became.

He had no phone in the car, and hours later he ran into another phone truck and discovered that we were far, far from the office and it was late, so we all went home. Neither of us mentioned the incident and we all got along pretty well after that. We learned later that the "disaster" at the building was that the inside floor mat was left outside!

Customers often turn molehills into mountains—scale them with tact.

Caught barefooted!

The biggest cleaning mysteries often have the simplest causes.

Out of the volumes of cleaning complaints we received over the years, one stands out as a classic. The first call came from a telephone building in a town 120 miles from our home office.

"This is the engineering department, Don."

"How are you doing?"

"Great. Listen, Don, we don't like to complain but for the second morning now, there are big barefoot prints all over the top of two of our desks."

"Barefoot tracks??"

"Yeah."

"Ah, there couldn't be. How could barefoot tracks be on top of an executive desk?"

On the first two identical calls like this, I talked them into believing something must be wrong with them if they were seeing bare footprints on desks. We had a big laugh over it and figured the engineers must have been drinking the fluid out of their transients.

The third time they called, I began the same old line and the manager stopped me. "Dammit, Don, I tell you there were barefoot prints on three desks this morning. Now we aren't crazy—they are there every morning! Come see for yourself."

Intrigued by the situation and aware that it was perhaps time to do something about it, I told him Arlo and I were on our way to investigate. When we arrived the next day, they led us to the second floor and over to the desks and sure enough, there were good-size bare footprints all over them. We thought and reasoned and questioned, but couldn't come up with the answer. We decided that the only thing to do was to turn out all the lights, and hide in the engineering room to catch the culprit red-footed. I left Arlo to do this and went to do some other business with the telephone manager. When I returned at 10:30 P.M. Arlo was sitting big-eyed in the lobby. "The mystery is solved," he said.

We entered the dark room where Arlo gestured me over to the windows. Indeed the mystery was solved. The three-story building we were in was just four feet away from a big apartment building, so close you could shake hands from building to building. Directly across from the engineering section and the three desks was an apartment serving as a temporary dorm for college girls. As all of us witnessed, the coeds dressed rather informally in their off hours, bouncing around playfully in their skivvies (and some without), unconcerned with the dark, unoccupied building next door. The Varsity men who maintained the building were also students and red-blooded American boys. When they finished with their work, they must be turning off the lights and standing on the desks to get a better view. Anxious not to scratch their "bleachers," they took off their shoes. The tiny bit of powder they picked up from the freshly spray-buffed floor was enough, combined with the sweat from bare feet, to leave unmistakable tracks. Since they left in the dark, they never noticed them.

The two boys showed up about then, hustling around to get their cleaning done so they could enjoy their usual late-night show. Arlo pointed out the tracks and asked them how they got there. One muttered, "A ghost," the other, "Angels." Arlo then gave them a long lecture on trustworthiness and moral cleanliness and sent a note over to the girls' apartment suggesting the immediate installation of drapes or window shades.

We later found out the whole engineering department was mad at us for solving the mystery!

Angelfish on the rocks

Janitors get the blame for most of what goes wrong in a building, from stealing to fire and flood. One of the best examples of this happened in the coldest part of Alaska, at the Delta Junction school, a small old remodeled military building, underdesigned for the minus sixty below zero temperature outside. Even when the heat was on, any water dropped on the tile floor of the science room might freeze.

The teacher presiding over this classroom icebox was proud of the place, especially her five-foot high, two-foot-wide, all-glass aquarium of tropical fish. One night the furnace malfunctioned and failed. The next morning the aquarium was a miniature glacier. The glass had broken and dropped away, and all of the fish were suspended in a five- by two-foot block of ice. It was like a still-life aquarium. The fish had never been colder nor the words for the janitor hotter from those who loved the fish We never figured out whether we were being blamed for the furnace failure or the weather.

My name in lights!

There were some restrooms whose specs said we must clean every inch every night. Inspections there were difficult, until someone discovered the "black light." Once all the lights were out in a restroom, you just switched the magic light on (it was a purple strobelike thing—ultraviolet, or "black light") and any "misses" of uncleaned-up urine would gleam like a diamond. It was a real janitor killer.

I first encountered this on an inspection tour through a Bell building in Florida. It seems that our quality of service there had dropped in recent months and the Bell management, frustrated with trying to get their money's worth and prove our deficiencies, resorted to buying a suitcase full of crime detection material, including the black light and some "clue spray" that was invisible in ordinary lighting. They then sprayed the clue spray on various parts of the floor, restroom fixtures, walls, etc., a week or so before I arrived. When the preliminary chitchat was over, I could see that the Department Chief and Contract Administra-

tor woro bursting at the ocamo to take a little tour. On the tour I
was the main billing. We would walk into a restroom, turn out
the light, turn the black light on, and in beautiful green glow-
ing fluorescent my name, D-O-N (printed as neatly as a phone
man with a spray can could manage), appeared on the sides of
women's restroom stall walls, the underside of toilet seats, and
the like. I never thought I'd hate to see a three-letter word worse
than a four-letter one in a restroom, but it happened. We were
had—the evidence of uncleaned places blinked out at us like a
Las Vegas billboard.

One day five of us big wheels were using a black light to
inspect a women's restroom after our own crew cleaned it. We
all went inside and flipped off all the lights, but when we tried
to turn on the black light it wasn't working. Suddenly a woman
came into the restroom and turned on the light switch, and there
all five of us were, huddled in a circle in the dark. "My word,"
she said, and whirled and ran. I never dared ask what the gossip
was around the office that day and didn't want to know.

Traps for the unwary

*A well-designed professional inspection system
will tell any client or contractor what he wants to
know far better and more reliably than traps.*

Many building managers we worked for had a hard time telling if a place was really cleaned or not, and so resorted to setting "traps" around—in other words hiding little objects under, over, and behind things, and then the next morning, after everything had been cleaned, they would rush in to see if any of the planted items were still there. If they were, this was perfect proof that the janitor didn't do his job.

You can't clean every square inch of a million square foot office building every night—it would cost a billion dollars a year to clean. There is an acceptable middle ground in all things, including cleaning, however many paranoid building managers never learned this. They would call us in the next morning, gloating, open their hands and reveal two paper clips, one marked toothpick, a nail-polish-dotted nickel, and an initialed aspirin. It was instant trial and conviction.

I remember one night in one of the big medical center buildings in Vegas (all doctors' and other medical professionals' offices and labs). Dennis Parker, our manager, took me in with him for an evening cleaning. As we walked into the elevator he bent down and picked a match out of the elevator track. He held it up to me and said, "Plant." "You're paranoid," I said. "No," said he, giving me a closeup view. "Notice the end has been sharpened with scissors and there is a tiny date on it." Sure enough, some doctor (probably billing you for the time) took twenty minutes to prepare and position this little trap. As we walked down the hall Parker reached around the coffee machine without even looking and snatched up the broken tine of a plastic fork. "Plant," he said. "There is one every night." It was hilarious—we went through the whole building and he knew right where they all were and collected a handful of little traps. Then spreading them all out on a credenza, he said, "You know, Don, this building is full of doctors who have state-of-the-art stethoscopes but would never even know if you cleaned the building or not. They can't tell clean from dirty. Once the traps are removed we could all just go home." And he was right.

I remember one job where the contract specified daily dusting. A manager hid a lid on a ledge up above eye level, and every night we lifted the lid up, dusted under it, and set it right back. It drove the guy crazy; he could never find any dust to complain about and yet the lid was never gone. I haven't told him to this day and decades later, he is probably still wondering.

Some complaints had class. For three days our people missed some areas and a corner or two, and when the Western Electric manager's note about it got no response, he resorted to wit. The next day as we were sweeping by, there seemed to be a neat little piece of paper with something written on it lying on the floor. Upon closer examination, it was a tiny funeral tent, with a little cross and a message: "Here lies Carl Cockroach—he died on this spot four days ago and is still lying there."

We got the message... and the cockroach in the future.

The trail of blame

When disaster strikes, janitors are always the first to be implicated. We cleaned a State Farm complex in the L.A. area, where instead of a person to pick up the mail they had an over-weight robot, Harry, who probably cost more than twenty mail people. Harry was programmed to travel throughout the building and gather papers in his little automated arms. To help guide Harry, a trail (line) was sprayed on the carpet, a clear, invisible conductive material called "Robatrac." When Harry was clicked on he would follow the line.

Our contract called for shampooing the carpet quarterly, and we did it, totally unaware of the Robatrac. We were using some killer-diller super carpet cleaner in the heavily trafficked mailroom, and had to go over the carpet many times to get it clean. We finally did, but unbeknownst to us we also dissolved—removed—the Robatrac there.

The next morning, Harry came chugging down the hall as usual but when he turned into the mailroom (then occupied by a shapely female) he had no guide path and literally "hit on" the lass—pinned her in the corner, his little clasping hands reaching for female this time instead of mail! The State Farm executives, sensing a harassment lawsuit, said "The janitor did it." (They thought we'd reprogrammed Harry as a joke, when all we'd done was innocently try to do a good job on the carpet!)

They finally realized they needed to reprogram Harry, and give better instructions from then on to the carpet shampooers.

The case of the carousing crows

Sometimes, no matter how good your cleaning service, you just couldn't win. Our big Hewlett-Packard contract in Corvallis, Oregon, seemed like a sweet one. It was a nice building, the owners paid to keep it immaculate, and we had the programs and staff to do it. But there were a couple of beautiful flowering trees in the courtyard landscaping, that in the fall produced a small crabapple-like fruit. The crows in the area found these irresistible and cleaned up all of the fallen fruits for us. However after the fruit fell it fermented quickly, and the crows always seemed to have had one too many. They would fly up to the roof, and too drunk to realize that the large strips of rubber caulking up there were not big worms, would grab and yank out sections of caulk, ruining the roof. Then they would stagger around on the roof trying to balance themselves with only half a brain, slide down the roof, and fall several stories to the ground. The building manager screamed at us for letting their caulk get ripped out, and all of the bird lovers in the building screamed at us to do something about the poor crows that were falling off the roof. I don't remember what we did to remedy the situation. I think we hid!

Bummed out!

Janitors are often asked to fix not only cleaning problems—but those of the human race as well.

One of cleaning clients' most common complaints was running out of toilet paper. Even when you tried to make a scientific study of people's habits in a given place (how often they used the restroom, and which stalls), and installed double rolls in the most frequently used stalls, you never could absolutely prevent this.

One time when we were cleaning at the Grand Canyon during tourist season we were really hopping to it, hoping to make a good impression on the Parks and Recreation people. In the restroom, which had enough stalls to resemble the starting gate at Santa Anita racetrack, at 7 A.M. we had every toilet paper holder newly loaded, enough to last three or four days, we thought. At 9 A.M. that same day came the famous call, "No toilet paper in the restroom!" Impossible!

Nope, sure enough a quick inspection confirmed that every single roller was bare. An old park veteran saved us a desperate call to Scotland Yard. It was a little element of thievery. The hikers, headed to the bottom of the canyon and anticipating a pit stop in the bushes on the way down, would raid the restrooms before they left, unrolling a generous handful of paper or if a roll was smaller, taking the whole thing. What a bummer—back to the drawing board!

The mystery of the missing gummy bear

Speaking of thievery, my whole regional management staff was called into the office of a major company once and confronted with the fact that our employees were stealing. Their manager led us into a corner office and introduced us to the occupant, an engineer who had made the complaint. "What is missing?" his manager asked him. Pouting, the man pointed to a large bowl of hard candy on the corner of his desk. "There!" he said. "They took a piece of my candy." Looking at the 200-plus remaining pieces, we all had the same question in mind: "How could you possibly know one piece is gone?" So we asked about this and the victim said, "It wasn't the hard candy, it was the cinnamon bears. They ate one of my cinnamon bears." Again the manager asked him how he knew. "Because...," answered the accuser, now getting emotional, "cinnamon bears are my favorite and I counted them. There were twelve lined up around the edge when I went home and only eleven when I returned."

Good Lord—what could you say? Our janitor, in a moment of temptation, probably did snatch up and devour one of the bears. Can you believe it? This engineer with nothing more to do than line up cinnamon bears wanted to fire a humble, hard-working janitor. We had to make a 300-mile drive on icy roads to hear this.

Janitor justice

There are politics in complaints, too!

Most managers of the companies we worked for were top people, considerate and fair. However, we've all known and maybe even worked for a few bullies and intimidators. With those the impulse to someday get even can burn like a pilot light in back of a janitor's mind for quite a while.

In one large building we cleaned, two of the department heads, one a man and the other a woman, I was sure had taken and gotten "A's" in "How to Make Janitors Miserable 101." The other departments loved us, but these two, for years, ragged us constantly. Our rating in that building was the highest in the whole Bell System, yet still these folks kept trying to hang us. They griped and complained, left insulting notes, bragged that they were "hard to please," talked sharply to our people, and in general bullied us.

One Friday evening there was a basketball game and we, the crews, all went, and so didn't clean the building at our usual time slot of 6-9 P.M. After the game, we went out to dinner, and then after midnight, when the building was dark and abandoned, we went down to clean. Flinging open the doors of the ladies' lounge down in the basement, we interrupted an intimate couch scene, starring none other than those two unpleasable department heads (who were both married... to other people). We backed out with a quick, "Excuse me!" We knew we didn't need to clean that room right now.

Talk about a miracle! You cannot believe how clean their parts of the building suddenly got. Neither ever complained again and for the next few months we always had to suppress a smile when sweeping by them.

Another time, we had a contract to apply a strong and long-lasting weedkiller (it was called "sterilant") to a communications equipment site. We'd bought six sacks of it for this job, and were waiting to work it into our schedule (until we were going to be in the area). Meanwhile, the "know it all" and very impatient manager of the building called us every day. "When are you going to do this job?" We were going to do it soon, but no hurry, since it wasn't an emergency. He wouldn't let up, and since applying sterilant to the ground was simple—just spread it like fertilizer or lawn seed—he proceeded to do the job himself one afternoon. He read the instructions and sprinkled the white granular stuff (overgenerously) on the site. He should have read

ALL of the instructions. Step 2 was to wet the sterilant down well with water so it dissolved and was absorbed into the area where it was applied. He didn't. There was a gully-washing rain that night and all of those undissolved granules flowed down to the adjoining property of a fantastic green thumb, a doctor whose hobby was rare and ornate trees, plants, and shrubs. The amount of sterilant the manager applied to the tower site was enough to kill concrete, so you can imagine what it did to Dr. Green's landscape.

Once it dissolved in the next rain, it killed everything. The manager's company had to come in with backhoes, loaders, and dump trucks and remove all of the contaminated soil and replace it, up to six feet in places. Even after that growing anything there was difficult. On our next visit to the manager's building we never mentioned it, but we noticed he wasn't too quick to take over any of our projects after that.

Reading all of the instructions is something many of us consider somehow unnecessary.

The janitor fights back

Venting even the most righteous indignation directly is rarely a good idea or benefit in business.

It was always hard to discipline employees for things you secretly wished you could do. Once in a while the picked-on, beat-down janitor just snapped and turned on his or her tormentors.

The chop

This faithful Varsity worker had just finished a rugged shift cleaning a bigger mess than usual. Figuring he had given the job his best possible effort, he was passing the large marble-topped security desk in the lobby of the building on his way out, when a complaint note was handed to him that said, "The wrong color toilet paper has been installed on Floor #2." Infuriated by the petty nature of the complaint, he karate-chopped the inch-thick marble slab, breaking it in two, much to the astonishment of the guard and spectators. No one felt moved at that moment to demand any further adjustments in the color of the toilet paper.

The mop

One of our top cleaners, Samolee, an immigrant from South America, worked in a downtown office building. Stripping and waxing floors is brutally hard work and Samolee, a meticulous floor expert, had after ten exhausting hours just applied a sparkling final finish coat of wax with a mop. The big room had two entrances, one that led to a dry, clean floor, and the other right to the freshly coated area. Samolee waxed to that door, and stood proudly as his wax, now just getting tacky, started to dry to perfection.

A woman returning from a break approached the door to his freshly waxed masterpiece, and bowing politely to her, he said, "Please, Madam, would you use the other door?" It was only fifty feet away, and actually closer to her workstation. She sneered, made a disrespectful remark, and brushed past him, leaving unrepairable tracks in the tacky finish. Samolee snapped, bellowed a Tarzan-like yell, raised his mop like a lance, and charged the woman, laying his final coat of wax on that job atop the woman's head. A 36-ounce mop full of wax is weighty, so the woman did not remain upright. We had to dismiss Samolee, but he was a fallen hero executed in behalf of our many years of urges to do the same.

The pour

Tom, finishing a tough all-night shift of cleaning after the public, was driving his Varsity van back to the shop through heavy morning traffic. His patience, near the limit, finally reached an end when an aggressive driver pulled in front of him, stealing his rightful position in the lane, and then started chatting with a friend who pulled up alongside him as traffic stopped for a light. Tom got out of his van, opened the side door, and removed a 5-gallon bucket of floor wax. He walked up to the offender's car in front of him and poured the wax on the astonished driver's windshield and hood. We didn't charge Tom for the wax, and the victim probably couldn't read Tom's plate number through the waxed window. Tired janitors can be touchy!

CHAPTER 8

Selling Cleaning to the World

Cleaning—forever a hard sell

AS TIME went on, I became a popular speaker for community and church groups, especially on the subject of cleaning. I eventually put together an entertaining three-hour "cleaning concert" showing home cleaners how to clean like the pros, and presented it in person across the West, and eventually the country.

The response to this so convinced me of the need for information for home cleaners that I wrote (at age 45) a book called *Is There Life After Housework?* and self-published it. Before long the national publisher Writer's Digest Books took it on, and helped to make it a bestseller, which resulted in some nice profits for both of us. (For a time it was even ahead of *The Joy of Sex* and *30 Days to a Beautiful Bottom* on the bestseller list!)

Doing publicity for this book put me on the media circuit, and I did thousands of TV and radio appearances before I was through, plus interviews for just about every major newspaper in the U.S., and chalked up two million plus air miles! I wrote over thirty more books afterward, resulting in many paid speaking jobs across the country, and promoting me, eventually, to a major spokesperson for cleaning, in fact, "America's #1 Cleaning Expert."

Even with that title, I had a big, big marketing job ahead of me. When "I don't do windows" is a statement people make with pride, parents use cleaning as a threat or punishment for misbehavior, and cleaning for a living is seen as a dead-end job, you have your work cut out for you!

"Would you want him at your house?"

Even a cleaner from Idaho could grab some share of respect and fame from adults. The kids, good for them, don't take fame, wealth, or media hype at face value.

One day I received a call from a group of church women who said they had heard I did cleaning seminars free for church groups; could I do one for them in Willard, Missouri? I told them I'd be glad to if and when I was close by, but a trip there alone would mean two days of travel time and $1000 in expenses. Six months later I did a speaking job in Kansas City. That wasn't so far away, so I called them and told them to get a place and a crowd and I'd take the stage. When I showed up they said there was no hotel or motel in town, so the whole church got together and drew straws. The short straw got me. A red-haired mother of six, Mrs. Harris, drew it. She was terrified to have "America's #1 Cleaning Expert" staying at her home. When I got there, there wasn't a live germ anywhere. They'd even cleaned inside the faucets!

The seminar was at a school, there was a big crowd, and my hostess Mrs. Harris had the job (assigned before the great straw-drawing) of introducing me. Halfway through her introduction she stumbled a bit trying to tell about me, and a few titters and guffaws issued from the audience. She was so nervous she was almost in tears, and in a loud voice she burst out, "Well, if you think it's so funny you ought to have him staying at your house!"

The crowd roared and I was on. That evening at her home (after a bunch of calls to my secretary to find my favorite everything) she served a first-class dinner, including a raspberry dessert that I'd have sold my birthright for! It was a perfect, very successful evening, and she pointed out a beautifully prepared, spacious bedroom afterward and said goodnight. I sighed and got ready to crawl into that big lovely bed. But no matter how I tried, I couldn't get into it and couldn't figure out why. I was forty-eight years old, and had heard about "short-sheeted" beds, but the real thing was intriguing to the point of frustration. Finally I had to dismantle "the perfect bed" and remake it so I could get to sleep.

Next morning (Saturday), I came down for breakfast and all the kids were in suits and ties and dresses for me. Mrs. Harris, still a little nervous, was surely counting the minutes till my exit. She politely asked me how I'd slept. "Fine," I said. Then the little four-year-old piped up, "Was it hard to get into bed?" All of the kids giggled, and Mrs. Harris' face turned white, then red— she knew immediately what they had done. I left cheerfully, but I'll bet those kids got a long, long lesson in bedmaking!

We were on a seminar trip and I'd done my three-hour presentation the night before in Blanding, Utah. It was Valentine's Day and my wife and I were getting ourselves ready for a long motor trip to another show the next night. There was a knock on the door, and when my wife opened it, in streamed sixteen bubbling, enthusiastic women with trays of Valentine goodies, praising and thanking me for the show. We could hardly get them to leave! My wife turned to me and said, "Well, every man's dream—seventeen women in your motel room and it's legal!" Another of the little rewards of being in the cleaning business.

Fast talking

Humor and liveliness will excuse a fair number of shortcomings.

Hustle! Hustle! Hustle! Guess I learned it playing ball. To make up for lack of size, coordination, or skill, I ran harder, moved faster, and even began to talk faster. There followed a lifetime of my mind being ahead of my mouth. I was notorious for half-sentences, jumping from one subject to another, leaving out words, combining words, and inventing words, and it only seemed to get worse with age.

In the seminars or "cleaning concerts" I gave all over the country, I was always trying to get eight hours of instruction into three hours, so I talked fast and used lots of visual aids. My rapid-fire approach to seminar presentations could sometimes be as confusing to the audience as trying to condense all of these janitor stories into a little book was for me. When a full-day floor care seminar is squeezed down into a 15-minute "short course," for instance, both parties have to strain a bit. One woman, in tears, was comforted by another who had attended an earlier seminar and recorded it. "Don't worry," she said, "I took the recording home and played it on worn-out batteries and it came out just right!"

Southerners had the most trouble, since they usually talk slooooow. It often took three minutes for them to get a question asked. "Mr. Azslett… what do you do with all the flaws?" "The what?" "The flaws," the woman would slowly drawl out.

"Flaws in what?" I'd ask back.

"The flaw—you know, the flaw you walk on."

"Oh, you mean the floors!"

Another would ask, "Mr. Azslett, how do y'all get rid of 'raid mood.'"

"Is that a roach killer?" I'd ask.

"Noooo—'raid mood.'"

With the help of an interpreter, I found out she meant "red mud."

My speaking speed did allow an outstanding amount of information to be conveyed in a short time, which was appreciated by most. It also got me in some embarrassing "slip of the tongue" situations. My theory and demonstration of cleaning second-story bedroom windows was always, "They don't have to be immaculate or be cleaned too often because from the outside, since they're two stories up, no one can really see them anyway, and in the daytime everyone is busy working elsewhere and who looks out the bedroom window anyway?" I was speaking to a large group of church women and presented a similar philosophy: "As far as the inside of your bedroom windows, don't worry. When the drapes are pulled you should be too busy to look out the window anyway." A great roar of laughter came from one of the bolder listeners, and her comment card later asked, "Where have you been all my life?"

I guess the height of confusion came when I did a seminar in Twin Falls, Idaho. In the audience were two young deaf women and their sign language translator. Her hands were almost a blur trying to keep up with me, and when my words and sound effects were things like: "geepee-geepee-geepee" (my approximation of the sound of a dry squeegee blade going across a window), "twinky," "el gunko," and "scrubbee-scrub-scrub," she would glance at me in desperation. Meanwhile, the two women she was translating for laughed and their eyes sparkled, so I figured they must be gaining something from it all. The weary translator trudged up to me afterwards and awarded me and my subject matter the honor of being
the most difficult ever to sign.

Foot in mouth... or bowl?

Don't underestimate your audience's intelli-gence—they often know more than you do!

"How many of you have a ring in your toilet?" was a question that always got a lot of raised hands from my eager cleaning audiences. "Well don't worry, folks, there is nothing wrong with you—this is caused by the water in the bowl evaporating and the remaining minerals sticking to the side of the bowl at the water line." They would nod in understanding. This was my big moment now—I'd show them the professional secret for the sturdy old-style porcelain bowls; the wonderful, feather light, safe, and effective pumice stone.

I held it up like a Babe Ruth candy bar as I sang its praises and then did a demo with it, using it to remove a toilet ring. I did this for more than a year, and one night in Hawaii a little Japanese woman raised her hand. "Mr. Aslett, can you use these on your feet?" Believe this or not, though I was a farm boy and probably had plenty of corns and callouses, I had never seen or heard of pumice being used to remove them. So when she asked this question I assumed maybe she was a little finicky about putting her hand in the toilet and wanted to somehow use the pumice with her foot. So I tried to explain how she might do this with one foot in the toilet, with the pumice perhaps tied to her foot. I thought I was giving a serious answer to a question, but she thought I was making fun of her, and the audience thought the whole thing was hilarious.

Several in the audience, sensing the confusion, shouted out, "No, Mr. Aslett, she wants to use the pumice on her foot!" "I know," I said, and continued to explain that sticking your foot in the toilet was no better or easier than sticking your hand in the toilet. By now the place was in an uproar and people were showing me their feet and gesturing wildly—I told them that a pumice bar would probably fit any foot. Someone yelled out, "Corns and calluses!" and I said I doubted the pumice would be on there long enough to cause them. Anyway, it was like a ten-minute game of ring around the conversation, and I felt like I ought to crawl into the toilet when I finally realized what was up. I did recover slightly by darting down into the audience and giving the woman a pumice bar—for both her feet and under the toilet seat!

Reserve on the reservation

Don't ignore cultural differences—they can make a big difference in how things are perceived... and received.

One day, I received a request from a BIA (Bureau of Indian Affairs) agent who decided my ability to teach and inspire housework skills would benefit the Native Americans living on the Fort Hall Indian Reservation near Pocatello. I accepted, and showed up with my squeegees, sponges, and most sparkling wit.

Teaching Native Americans for the first time was a surprising experience—not until years later, working with them and having some live in our home as foster children, did I understand their temperament and culture, humor, and spiritual insight. That day all of the available Shoshone and Blackfoot had been rounded up in a crowded conference room. Most of them had no idea what this paleface pow-wow was about or why they were here.

At the very front, eight feet from my model demo house, sat a row of the most perfect pureblood Indian grandmothers I'd ever seen. Their dark, wrinkled faces mapped 75 to 90 years of dignity. They were stunningly handsome and noble-looking women, but remained entirely expressionless during my entire rip-roaring cleaning snake oil show. There was not a movement or reaction from one of them the whole time. I could feel their eyes on me, but what they were thinking was impossible to tell. My best and funniest stories and examples, which normally sent crowds into hysterics, got zero reaction. I was sure they spoke English.

During my long and unrewarding delivery of the gospel of cleaning, once or twice I caught a two-second flicker of a smile from a couple of the younger and more modern-looking women. While I was packing up my gear, a husky Indian attendee came up to me politely and said, "You are good, white man, but you try too damn hard."

Welcome to the big time!

Very mundane things can make a big difference in how things come out, so when it really counts, check and re-check.

It was early Sunday morning, and a neighbor's cow stuck its head through our bedroom window, chewing its cud. A sure sign that things were going to be eventful! I seldom travel on the Sabbath, but had to leave that Sunday at noon for my first-ever book promotion tour. Air service out of my home city of Pocatello was limited to a few small "prop" planes at odd hours, so my wife Barbara drove me to the Salt Lake airport, two hours away. Armed with my stunning new set of housework props in a big brown leather suitcase, I said good-bye and was off to San Francisco, scheduled the next morning to do the famous KGO "AM San Francisco" live TV show, followed by others through the day. I was sure that I had no equal for subject matter—what could beat cleaning!

I was really psyched to do my tour well, so I was in my best suit by 7 A.M. the next morning, determined to be at the studio early. I wanted to put a notebook in with my props and so heaved the leather bag onto the bed and unzipped it. My first thought was, "What's this old girdle doing in my suitcase?" Then I pounced and pawed like a frantic gopher, but there were no props. I grabbed the tag and it read "Harriet Reynolds, Anchorage, Alaska." Surely I was dreaming. I wasn't. This couldn't happen to me—only numbskulls take the wrong bag! I could see the end of my great TV career flashing before my eyes. I was sunk. The San Francisco airport was forty minutes away, and it was rush hour.

I dove for the phone, got two slow talkers at the airport and then the freight department. Then a silence followed a promise to see if my bag was there. I spelled out my predicament, telling the man at the other end that I was a famous TV star, scheduled to go on KGO AM in forty-five minutes. He understood, and said a delivery boy had left there at 7 A.M., five minutes ago, but he thought he could catch the truck. He caught it. I sat in a cab in front of the hotel with the erroneously claimed Anchorage bag, holding my breath as I waited for the deliveryman. It was 7:45, 7:46, 7:47... I had to be at KGO at 8 A.M. and live TV shows don't wait. Now it was 7:48, 7:49, 7:50. He came! I tipped him $25, switched cases, and told the cabbie I was James Bond and there was a bomb in the suitcase due to explode at 8:01 if I wasn't out of his cab (not a joke you would dare to make today). As a result, I can say I've ridden down the hills and streets of San Francisco at more than sixty miles an hour—I left fingernail gouges in his door handle.

At 8 A.M. I walked through the door of KGO, calm and collected, at least on the outside. The show went well—a real pro named Cheryl interviewed me and much to the audience's delight graciously dodged my waving bowl brush. They wanted me back! I packed my gear (met Jane Fonda in the quiet room) and caught a cab to an interview with the "Home" writer for the *San Francisco Examiner*, who to my surprise was fascinated by my toilet tales. I got a full-page spread in the *Examiner*, and also did interviews with magazines, radio and TV stations all over town.

When I finished that evening, exhausted but exuberant, the cab dropped me at the Sir Francis Drake Hotel (I was a little disappointed that the cab driver didn't recognize me). I'd missed three meals, but was reluctant to go to a restaurant for fear of autograph seekers and the press, so I pulled my coat collar up and headed to a Chinese food takeout stand a few blocks away. The streets were teeming with people—any minute I knew somebody would yell out, "It's him—the Toilet Man!" and I would be inundated. But no one did, so I let my collar down and still had no more action than the parking meters; so then I took my coat off and carried it so no one could mistake that grey suit and squeegee tie pin I'd worn on the show! I whistled a cleaning song and inspected some dusty pictures—still no reaction. So I took my famous book *Is There Life After Housework?*, with its bright yellow cover, out of my coat pocket and carried it in full view, but not one single person even glanced at me, even as I waited twenty minutes in line. Armed with a couple of egg rolls, I headed back to the hotel. Frankly, I was appalled at how chicken-hearted those San Franciscans were, afraid to approach a famous figure.

Six blocks later, absent any admirers, I stood at the last light across from the hotel. I felt a tap on my shoulder and turned to face a lovely, classy woman. Finally she spoke, "Had a tough day, didn't you, handsome?" I sucked in my stomach, deepened my voice, and replied, "Yes, those studio lights and television shootings really take it out of you." (I was basking in my first fan club member.) "How would you like some nice warm company in your room tonight?" My fame bubble popped quickly. All I attracted with my brilliant performance in San Francisco was... a prostitute!

I ate my egg rolls alone, figuring Detroit, the next stop, would have greater appreciation for an authentic cleaning artist like me. Thirty days later, a veteran of a 15-city tour, no one (ladies of the house or evening) sought me out. In fact, in three years I did 1500 splendid appearances in the U.S. and at least 100 elsewhere, and still never had to hide from a mob of fans.

Enjoy the spotlight if it shines on you, but be aware that few people notice our moment in the limelight as much as we do.

From "The Toilet Man" to "The Dean of Clean!"

As a well-known professional cleaner, I've been christened with quite an array of nicknames. In my early housecleaning days, I was referred to as "that cleaning guy;" I soon moved up to being called "the Varsity man." Then because of my tendency to use toilet parables in my teaching and humor, I became "The Toilet Man."

It was really the media who began giving me clever titles to give my appearances on TV and radio and in print a little zap. "Porcelain Preacher" was the first, "the King of the Toilet Ring," "Duke of the Dustpan," and the "Dean of Clean" soon followed, then "Billy Graham of the Pine Sol Set," it never ended.

Finally one source suggested that I was unquestionably America's #1 Cleaning Expert. The title seemed to stick so I adopted it and have used it ever since. I'm sure there are some out there more technically knowledgeable about cleaning and its chemistry and economics, but there is probably no one who has embraced cleaning more wholeheartedly as not just a science and profession, but a lifestyle, a culture, and almost a religion.

Whenever I am called "the cleaning expert" I always point out to hosts or editors that "X" is an unknown quantity and "spurt" is a drip under pressure. No doubt the pressures of survival in this "low image" and highly competitive profession have forced some expertise out of me!

I've often been asked for the full list of my nicknames, so here it is.

The Porcelain Preacher
Billy Graham of the Pine-Sol Set
Ajax Evangelist
King of the Toilet Ring
The Pied Piper of Purification
The Fastest Bowl Brush in the
    West
Duke of the Dustpan
Baron of the Biffy
Dean of Clean
Minstrel of the Mop
Urinal Colonel
Guru of the Loo
Jet Set Janitor
Flush Gordon
Housecleaner Extraordinaire
Titan of the Toilet Bowl

The Cleaning Man
The Toilet Man
Don Juan of the John
Sultan of Shine
Czar of Cleanliness
Crusader for Clean
Squire of the Squeegee
Dean of the Dustbusters
Janitor Summa Cum Laude
Hercules of Housecleaning
The Clown Prince of Clean
The Wizard of Ooze
The Phyllis Diller of Toilets
Monsieur of Messes
Lee Iacleaner of the
    Corporate Toilet Bowl
Will Rogers of the Restroom

The true case of the toilet suitcase

A bold, imaginative approach can often turn a negative into a positive.

Several years of travel revealed to me that many of my fellow travelers had luggage that identified their profession. The cowboy had boot silhouettes on his clothes bag; the engineer, a transit case; the musician his violin case; baseball players had athletic bags; and look how much attention all the pilots get trailing their compact little flight bags down the concourse. Being #1 in the #2 business, I figured I should call some attention to my profession in my travels and in conversation often said I would be carrying a toilet suitcase someday.

Earl Parrish, one of our Florida area managers, and an expert in fiberglass molding, heard my comment and during my next trip there I was presented a perfect fiberglass toilet suitcase (or Stoolsonite, as I liked to call it).

As soon as I had it, I made up a business card that read:

Hi... I'm Don Aslett! I'm from Pocatello, Idaho. You're probably wondering about my strange luggage. It's not a porta-potty as it may appear; it's my suitcase. Why do I carry a toilet suitcase?

Well, doctors carry their little black bags, lawyers and business executives carry their attaché cases, and I, a professional janitor, carry a toilet suitcase.

The toilet which I (along with eight million other professional cleaners and fifty million home cleaners) clean regularly is a symbol of my trade. I carry it to dispel any doubt as to how I feel about my profession—I'm proud of it.

My toilet suitcase became my trademark as I traveled all over the country. It was a real attention-getter, and the media loved it. I would always close my cleaning seminars or convention speeches on the subject of the image or status of the cleaner and do a whole standup (or sitting down in this case—right on my toilet suitcase) comedy routine about getting respect for the business I was in.

I had a lot of fun with my toilet suitcase over the years. When I reached in to get a business card, no one wanted to shake hands with me afterward. The curious would ask, "What's in there?" I'd answer confidently, "My toilet articles."

I took it into a hotel once and the desk attendant assured me that this was a first-class hotel and there was no need to bring my own.

One intrigued bystander shouted across the terminal once, "You sure come prepared, don't you!" Another yelled out, "Bet carrying that around really poops you out!"

I was approached often by cross-legged kids, "Hey, does that really work?"

Looks always turned friendly when the elevator jammed and I had my toilet suitcase with me.

If you walk into the lobby of a hotel like the Waldorf-Astoria carrying a realistic-looking toilet, you will find that their speedy check-in policy is upgraded to instant—you are out of there and into a room *fast!*

I used to love going through upscale hotels like the Boston Marriott with my toilet suitcase. I'd enter the elevator full of men in $500 suits, diamond stickpins in their ties, fine leather briefcases, and *Wall Street Journals* under their arms. No one would turn their head as I stood there with a life-size toilet in hand. But unbelieving eyeballs would shift slowly down to it, then dart rapidly ahead, pretending that they didn't see it, or didn't know what it was. But if they paid $250 for their room as I did, they surely had one in there!

The crowd gathered around any airport luggage carousel would suddenly come alive when the conveyor belt spit out my "suitcase." Often a kid would yell, "Look, Mom—a toilet!" and then all kinds of remarks would ripple through the crowd as my white commode circled. "Can you imagine that?" "Must be a plumber." "Someone must really have to go a lot," etc. I let it circle a few times for maximum effect, and even some of those who had already retrieved their bags would wait to see... who.

Best of all, when my toilet suitcase came sailing through, I could safely ignore the sign that says, "Examine your luggage carefully: many bags look the same." When I did pick it off it was always in perfect condition, because it bore a sign on top of the lid that said, "If you break this, it will spill on you."

Once in a while my luggage didn't show up for a while, as on one flight to Seattle. When we (the airline agent, me, and other staff) finally tracked it down, we received a humorous, heartfelt apology that they (the pilots, flight attendants, and ticket counter) were so busy taking pictures of each other "enthroned" on it, they failed to get it on the flight.

I was on my way once to the "Sonya" show, a first-class program in Detroit rated up there with the Phil Donahue Show. I was told I would be met at the airport by a limousine and taken to my hotel. I slipped off the airplane wearing my red Scout coat (I'd left my good coat in Atlanta) and carrying an extension pole to use with a squeegee on the show. I guess I was pretty shabby looking for a TV celebrity. I walked through the lobby and there was a chauffeur with a sign saying "Sonya" with his eyebrows raised, scanning all of the nicely suited people. I walked up to him and he said, "I'm looking for a Mr. Aslett."

"I'm him," I said.

"Have you got your bags?" he said.

"They are coming," I replied.

"What do they look like?" he asked.

"The first one is blue and the second one is shaped like a toilet."

He looked down his nose at me and repeated the question: "*What* does the second one look like? You're putting me on, man!" He was a big, tall guy in a sharp dark suit with razor-sharp creases in the pants. He held his shoulders very straight and had a nicely trimmed beard—he was classy.

The blue suitcase came out first and I took it and stepped away from the carousel, while he stepped up to the carousel to wait. Suddenly there was a scream of laughter and jokes from the crowd, and I knew the toilet suitcase was coming. He glanced up and sure enough, there in all its splendor was my Stoolsonite, coming around the corner. The look on this man's face when it approached was worth the whole trip to Detroit. He started to perspire and his eyes searched from side to side to see if there was any way out. Every eye in the area was on the toilet

suitcase, wondering who would be uncouth enough to claim it. When it was about fifteen feet away he was actually squirming and flexing his fingers in pain. When it reached him he snatched it up as quickly as possible, gave me a sick look, and carried it to the limousine past the snickering crowd.

This was better than the cab driver in Pittsburgh who hauled me to the airport and sat there after we stopped and said, "Sir, would it really offend you if I didn't get out and take that toilet? I have friends in those other cabs."

It Really Happened! A Toilet Suitcase!

Fulfilling a five-year dream to own one, and two years of design, construction, and struggle by Varsity of the South to build one, a genuine, deluxe toilet suitcase was presented to Varsity's President by Earl Parrish from Varsity's Daytona Beach operation. The unit was constructed by Varsity managers with the help of a professional fiberglass boatmaker. It is light, durable, and as you can tell from the picture, entirely authentic looking.
—Scrubber's Scribe

"Mr. Aslett, with squeegee tie tack, white commode briefcase, outhouse-shaped leather folder, a stack of his books and rapid-fire, high-energy conversation, came well-armed for a recent Salt Lake City speaking engagement."
—The Salt Lake Tribune, April 6, 1992

"He's scrubbed thousands of toilets, taken 'pot shots' at people with a squirting toy toilet, and carries a toilet-shaped briefcase 'so everyone will hold their breath when I walk by,' he quipped."
—Barbara Wyman

A man in a woman's business

As I often tell my audiences, the biggest, ugliest housework problem in this country is that the majority of housework is caused by men and children—yet most home housework is done by women.

The question "Why is a man doing women's work?" was asked of me at least a thousand times, and it assumes, of course, that cleaning is a woman's job. The next question of "How does a man know anything about housecleaning?" was a direct challenge to my credibility.

Once the females found out that someone who cleaned for a living could provide some new and professional ways to cut cleaning, I was an icon, really the only man in recent history who had ventured publicly into (or out of) the traditional cleaning closet. Whenever I had the chance, I picked on the "non-cleaning" men unmercifully.

Even the most hardened feminist supported me, because my philosophy and seminars followed the spirit of the book I wrote for men titled *Who Says It's a Woman's Job to Clean?* I would often open my seminars (three hours of speaking to a mixed audience of men and women) by pointing out the pathetic tools most women had to use around the house—an antique vacuum that sprayed dirt all over the place, a warped pair of scissors you had to hold just right so they would cut, an old foot-treadle sewing machine, appliances with knobs and handles long gone—things they use every day, while at the same time the man has $220 torque wrench set (never used), a telescopic sight on his electric drill (used twice a year), and a deluxe $400 rifle (used once a year) in his closet. This was a performance I did with many antics. Women loved it, and the men slunk sheepishly down into their seats. One night at a seminar in Riverside, California, when I was "preaching" from the height of my compassion, one woman yelled "Yes!" and whacked her husband on the side of his head with her purse. The man took it, too—just shrank down in his seat.

Getting men to buy into the idea that cleaning and house care is a 50/50 deal is a hard sell, but one I haven't given up on and never will! One of the highlights of my campaign to reclassify "women's work" came when I was retained to speak at a convention of election precinct officials in Ohio. There were six hundred attending, mostly women. An ambitious local politician, Senator Robert Taft (directly related to President Taft) was the emcee of the event. He made all the right moves there until he introduced me and said, "You women are going to like Don Aslett because he will be talking about cleaning." A groan of disapproval issued forth from the audience, and Senator Taft was suddenly Senator Chauvinist. As I came on stage and past him slinking off I grabbed him by the arm, and asked loud enough for every last woman in the place to hear, "Senator, do you know what the 'housewife's revenge' is?" Puzzled, he said, "No."

"Well, Senator, men miss the toilet all the time, and no woman should ever have to clean a toilet, let alone the misses all over the side of the toilet, tub, and floor. (The audience applauded.) When your wife is on her hands and knees cleaning men's miss messes, she really hates you, so she reaches up on the vanity counter and gets a toothbrush! (The women began to laugh.) And guess whose toothbrush it is? (The Senator's face turned white, and the women roared in delight). "When she finishes scrubbing off that pee with your toothbrush, then guess what she does next, Senator?" (No answer, he's standing there like a shorn sheep.) "She rinses it out in the toilet and then puts it back. So if you occasionally have toilet breath, Senator, now you know the reason."

To help call attention to the cause of men helping more with housework, I've even made some special custom tools such as a lambswool duster with a golf club handle, a pancake spatula with a handle made from a Porsche gearshift, a dustpan with a tennis racket handle, and an iron with a handsaw handle. There is a long way to go yet, and slowly but surely society is grasping the idea that anyone of any gender can and should clean.

From mops to props

Our collection of clutter will usually tell more about us than we want anyone to know.

Once a TV segment was confirmed, it was always exciting. You had to hustle props to the set, because you wouldn't dare count on the studio staff to get the right stuff for the show. For my segments I often needed things like cat hair, fake dirt and dog poop, old engine oil, sawdust, mildew, hard water deposits, windows, and toilets, so we would tap every resource to gather the visuals. If the segment happened to be on removing stains we would prepare a carpet sample to challenge the host with mustard, tar, chewing gum, barf, or cigarette burns. After the show, we'd bring all of these props home and store them, knowing there would be a next time. I always wondered if I had a wreck or was searched on the way to the airport, what the police would think, trying to figure out what all of this could possibly be for. For my clutter presentations (which I did thousands of times on stage), I had a drawer full of all kinds of junk to snatch up and show the audience—ugly, tacky, broken, worn out, but familiar stuff people often keep.

On a trip to England, going through customs at Heathrow airport in London, a stern-faced officer asked me, "What's in the trunk?" "Junk, sir," I answered. "What do you mean, junk??" he questioned. I could see two other inspectors leaning over to listen and some of the crowd in line behind me, too, so I knew I had an audience gathering. "Okay, there's an empty paint can, broken sunglasses, padlock with no keys, broken fly swatter, defunct wristwatch, old bowling trophy, ten-year-old *National Geographic*, an ugly used shirt, a goat's brassiere, and other stuff." That set him back—all he could say was, "Anything else in there?" "As a matter of fact, yes sir, a toilet suitcase." His humorless lips tightened, "Open 'er up, chap."

By now everyone in viewing distance was looking and listening, and my wife, knowing what was coming, nudged me to just be serious so we could get through this without incident. I had done more than forty media appearances that trip in England and Scotland, and this was a sensational ending; someone demanding a show! I opened the big blue travel trunk, took out my toilet suitcase, and then removed a toilet eraser, toilet pencil sharpener, and a "Bowl Patrol" coat from it. The crowd, now more intrigued than impatient about the delay, loved it. Then the inspectors started through my junk drawer, pulling out an old distributor cap, warped trivet, empty Cool Whip container, cracked baby potty seat, etc. The customs officers (now two of them digging through my props) held up some of the stuff and said in a loud voice, "Why, this is just junk!" I smiled triumphantly as they "OK'd" me to repack and get back to the U.S.

Best dressed stress

Our performance is usually more important than our packaging.

In trying to elevate my appearance and image to "best dressed" status, I was a real failure. In my brief TV training the coach struggled to tell me nicely that even though somewhat similar, one dark blue and one black sock did not really match on camera.

I also never overcame my sporty, aggressive willingness to dive and tumble for the cause. I can put on a $500 suit and in fifteen minutes look like I've just changed a car tire without a jack. I often traveled with luggage that was oversize and overweight, and carrying it around always snagged clothes and stripped buttons. When the time came to wrestle with a kid, play a quick game of basketball, or let creative grandkids write on me, I always figured the experience was more valuable than the apparel. And of course the paint on my watch, under my fingernails, and in my ears seldom matched what I was wearing. Even after checking my luggage, I usually still toted a big clothes bag, my notebook, a briefcase with three or four manuscripts in it, a bulging pocket of miniature toilet keychains, and a five-foot squeegee extension handle. My colleagues made fun of me and my daughter gave me a copy of *Dress for Success*. My wife bought me an overcoat in an attempt to cover my disharmonizing colors. My parents bought me a fine sport coat for Christmas and I lost it the first evening I wore it (it was the first and only sport coat I'd ever owned).

Occasionally, after being around some slick Charlies, I would vow to refurbish my threads and enter the competition for "Best Dressed U.S. Male," but would never get near the semifinals. For Christmas in 1982, "A.M. Northwest" TV (which had an audience of over two million in Oregon, Washington, Montana, and Canada) asked me to do a thirty-minute three-segment appearance on "Carpet Care at Christmas." I had done two extremely successful shows with them previously, my books were on the bestseller list, and the Bon, a fine department store in the West, wanted me to appear, perform, and autograph at their stores. Figuring this called for a little more sartorial splendor than I usually exhibited (my newest suit was more than eight years old), I whipped down to the most upscale menswear store in Pocatello and challenged the clerk to upholster me for the Seattle invasion. I tried on a few two and three hundred dollar suits, then spotted a real beauty on the rack. It was, the salesman assured me, their finest, a Hickey Freeman. I hadn't heard that term since I was a teenager, when a friend of mine kissed his girl too hard on the neck. It was $525 with no vest, and only one pair of very snaggable-looking trousers—terrible—but considering my pending mob of admirers in the Northwest, I figured it was worth it. That suit, with my message and good looks, would surely put me ahead of Garfield on the charts. But it didn't.

A gorgeous twenty-nine-year-old buyer for the Bon hosted me on this trip, or tried to. I bumped my head getting into the car, dropped my clean overcoat in the gutter, and didn't have change for a tip. When I did get my coat on, the safety pin holding the lining in gleamed in the fancy hotel lights. When I coolly buttoned it (the only button left on it), the button popped off and rolled across the hotel lobby. Making a quick turn I knocked over a big Christmas display with a loud crash. Getting in the elevator, I poked a woman with my window-cleaning pole. When I got my schedule out of my briefcase, I didn't latch it securely, and when I picked it up to leave, all of the contents pitched out (pencils, scissors, tape, ruler, toilet keychains, Idaho potato pins, etc.). I outdid the famous bull in the china closet. Showing someone how to gracefully carry a rug cleaning machine, I struck the top of the door, and the handle snapped down and hit me on the lip, so then I had a fat, numb, bleeding lip to impress my fans.

It didn't stop when I yanked out my hotel key, and a Vitamin C tablet I carried rolled across the floor. Going home on the plane, I sat next to a beauty consultant from Max Factor—boy was she impeccable, absolutely a doll. Of course she had heard of me, the famous toilet writer, and I suavely opened my bag of Republic Air peanuts. Twice missing my mouth, the first peanut bounced down my front and onto the floor. I tried to coolly consume another, but it got loose and rolled to a stop by her hand. Finally I decided no one was even noticing my $500 suit, so I went back to my old $120 pinstripe and just got the job done.

Making cleaning more fun than sex

Don't advertise more than you're able to provide.

Although I took my responsibility to the media very seriously, I found most of them would resort to almost anything to get attention. As they often told me, when there is no news (no tragedy, flood, fire, crash, murder, or sensational adultery) to report for breaking news several times a day, they have to make news. One morning in a big CBS morning talk show news interview in Cincinnati, they opened the show with the fact that "Swale," a Kentucky Derby winning racehorse of the past, had died. When he broke for a commercial the anchorman turned to me and said dryly, "When you have to lead off with a dead horse, you know it is going to be a bad news day." I've since always marveled at how the local or national media can take nothing much and make it into the news of the day or evening—now that is talent and enterprise!

I did a noted TV talk show in San Diego once with three guests. I had the third and last segment. The host led off by interviewing two homosexual men who hugged and caressed for the whole segment. Next was a sex therapist who told the host he'd had sexual relations with 269 women (for professional reasons, of course) to investigate and help them adjust to their partners. Both of these were pretty racy interviews. Afterward the host (whom I'd worked with before) wiped his brow off camera and apologized. "Gee, Don, I'm sorry you have to follow that kind of subject—this is going to be tough." Boastfully I replied, "Listen, Frank, the day I can't make cleaning more fun than sex, I'm going to quit." Bad brag! When the commercial was over, he greeted viewers with, "Welcome back, folks. Now we have my friend Don Aslett, who will show us how to make cleaning more fun than sex."

I can't remember what I even did for that segment, but whatever it was, it worked. Two hours later I was paged for the first time ever in an airport, "Mr. Don Aslett, please pick up the white courtesy phone." It was Jo Hoff, publicist for my publisher Writer's Digest. "What did you do, Don? We're being flooded with calls for your new book, How to Make Cleaning More Fun Than Sex!" When I told my wife about it later that evening, she said, "Well, there's a title for a book that would really sell!" I decided to drop that approach and quit while I was ahead.

The right place and subject at the wrong time

Cleaning seldom makes a sensation, but it remains
a solid reality after the headlines fade.

I did two of my "Life After Housework" shows in the area of Charlotte, North Carolina, and an autographing was scheduled at a nearby Walden bookstore in a mall.

A table loaded with my cleaning books was placed perfectly, nudging out into the passing mall traffic. And was there traffic! However, 95% of those entering the store headed straight for my table and then right past it to plunk down $4.95 for the just-released Jessica Hahn issue of *Playboy*. You would have to see it to believe it, not only the number of these magazines bought but who bought them—saintly looking 65-year-old women, teachers, clerks, kids, and even the mall janitors all bellied up to the counter and carried out a bag containing the sizzling stories of Jim Baker's pulpit promiscuities.

One woman in her seventies waved the magazine at me, babbling on about how this was the first *Playboy* she'd ever bought (for the article, of course, not the pictures). A couple in their eighties came in, too, barely able to shuffle along, and then labored back out with their prize. A couple of ministers who stopped in did examine my books briefly, and some books about quilting on a nearby table, before quietly committing to magazine ownership.

While hundreds of *Playboys* went out, I sold one *Clutter's Last Stand* to a guilt-ridden husband (with his son) who had to buy something for his wife to make up for what he just bought. Some of the purchasers made it clear that it was not sex only that interested them; they had donated heavily to Jim and Tammy Baker and were looking after their investment.

No nostrils flared for my own writing efforts or subject—maybe housework and Hahn didn't mix. I was tempted to pose as Hugh Hefner!

While on tour for my twelfth book, *The Stainbuster's Bible*, one US Air stewardess, taking my ticket with a flirtatious sniff said, "Oh sir, I love what you are wearing!" I leaned close to her and whispered, "Paint thinner. I've just been removing tar from a carpet."

After seven straight shows with little time between them, I'd tossed all my solvents, bleaches, acids, alcohol, and a spotting cloth in my travel bag. If one of the drug dogs had sniffed my luggage it would have toppled over on its side and died.

The stain book tour took me up a notch in status. I was now approached like a doctor: "Doc, I have a stain right here...."

"Every time I clean my toilet, I think of you."

In publicity and the media your imagination is the only thing that penetrates the whole market.

The American dream has it that when you get really good at something—singing, dancing, swindling, acting, scoring points, writing or something—suddenly overnight everyone knows you, seeks your autograph, and showers you with potentially profitable propositions. It doesn't really happen that way.

Most of your moments of glory are short-lived, or have a less than silver lining. Like the time I was coming down the escalator from the gate at the Salt Lake City airport. The most attractive girl in the thirty or so ticket lines saw me, and let out a scream that caused everyone around to look hard. "Don Aslett! Oh, Don, I was thinking about you last night!" Both the onlookers and I were stunned at this romantic burst of recognition. Then as she reached me, she grabbed me by the arm and said, "Because my kid vomited on the carpet and it left quite a stain, I knew you'd know how to get it out." Everyone snickered gleefully as my expectations wilted.

I was constantly reminded what a hard sell "cleaning" is. No matter how humorous I made it or how many visual aids I used, how many funny cleaning stories I told, or how much fun I made it, it was still an uphill battle.

After one TV show when I was on tour for a book called *How Do I Clean the Moosehead?* it occurred to me that instead of showing the audience how to clean a moosehead if I showed them how to cook a moosehead, how to race moose, how to get elected to the moose lodge, or how to give a moose muting call, my ratings would have been higher.

The case of the reluctant cornstarch

"All in a day's work" (cleaning) sometimes means adventures that don't stop when an ordinary shift does.

Driving home from a funeral I spoke at one day, I said to my wife, "Boy, it would be nice to go to something just once where I wasn't running it, speaking at it, or responsible for paying for it. I'd like to just go and sit somewhere sometime as a spectator, no demands or pressure to 'deliver.'" The wand waved and I got my wish.

A publicist for the Eureka Company called and asked if I would be their "booth celebrity" at the National Housewares Show in Chicago. Truly heaven was calling. I'd wanted to see one of these shows for years, and now would be getting paid $1500 a day to do it, and staying all expenses paid in the most luxurious hotel in town. I was supposed to go and just stand there, nod, smile, absorb the goings-on and just relax and be worthless for a change.

When I got to Chicago, all three buildings of the enormous McCormick Center were full of buyers and sellers from all over the world. The miles of booths and displays were awesome, and the Eureka booth was not the usual 8' x 10' or so but fifty feet long, and it had a platform stage with a miniature living room at one end. The stage was my first clue that being an animated wooden Indian wasn't my destiny for these four days. One section of the "living room" had a 3' x 3' Plexiglas floor with a slanted mirror under it, so the audience could see under the rug (a clever idea, to demonstrate the vacuum's vigor and virtues). We would lift up the rug, sprinkle "dirt" (we used cornstarch for this) on the Plexiglas, and lay the carpet back over it. Then as we vacuumed the carpet, the cornstarch was sucked up through the rug, much to the delight of onlookers. The stage also had a new home carpet extractor and Eureka's new full-size cordless, battery powered vacuum. Red, sleek, and low, it was as sexy as any Corvette.

My job (it turned out I did have one) was to pull in potential buyers, especially from big places like Sears or Penney's. Eureka had hired a model (who certainly overshadowed any machine) to assist me. She ran my microphone and a big TV showing me doing Eureka commercials. While I beat the carpet she batted her eyes, sprinkled the cornstarch, and pointed at the demonstration with perfect fingernails.

I started each day at 8:30 A.M. and ended at 5 or 6 P.M., never leaving the booth—no food, no bathroom visits, no break, because you never knew when that all-important client or buyer might stop by. Right across from the Eureka booth was a blender demonstration where four blondes and a TV chef ground up ice, cabbage, and apples, and made pizzas. I'm here to testify that the average buyer, Neiman Marcus or Kmart, likes food more than a vacuum pitch.

Within fifteen minutes, my illusions of an easy job were gone. It was gut-hard work. Especially demonstrating a prototype machine when parts and clamps fell off or flew into the air, or the battery fell out while six prospective buyers were watching. As one customer was bending over to study the pressure valve connection on the extractor more closely (I'd never seen or used the machine before that day), I yanked too hard and the faucet fitting blew, drenching the fellow's fine suit. By the end of the first day, I felt like a carnival huckster, or one of the street solicitors in front of a porno shop trying to get people in.

By 6 that evening the Eureka executives were raring to go out on the town, and of course they wanted me (the "movie star") to go along. I'm not much for eating anyway and eating for three hours in a loud, smoke-filled environment was of zero interest to me. I assured them I had collected fifty business cards from their potential customers and needed to excuse myself and go write up my notes.

I dragged myself into my hotel room at 7 P.M., ordered a tuna fish sandwich and tomato juice, and started sorting contacts. My editor (we were finishing one of our first books for New American Library) called me and gave me an hour's worth of little assignments that had to be completed quickly. I sold vacuums all night in my sleep.

Up again at 6 A.M. and back to the sales floor. Every day got tougher. That ice-chipping blender and the smell of pizza drove me crazy, and it was hard to rally a crowd to stand and listen to you selling a vacuum.

Later that day, I was demonstrating for our biggest audience so far, a platoon of Japanese businessmen, with cameras and note pads at the ready and reeking of money, who might be willing to join an American success. Beauty spread the cornstarch and helped the beast inform them that I would indeed suck the deep down "dirt" from the rug. Polite nods followed; and the sound of clicking Nikons. I started up the vacuum and went into my routine, when a look of horror came to the face of my lovely assistant. She was looking at the mirror under the floor, and began mouthing a silent SOS. I finally decoded her dramatics enough to realize that the cornstarch (fake dirt) was not moving. I smiled, bent down, and adjusted the vacuum a notch closer to the rug and continued. Her look of panic was now pain, so I raised the suction another notch. The cornstarch continued to stay put. In desperation I dropped the vacuum all the way to the face of the carpet, giving that innocent little rug full power. The vacuum picked the rug right up off the floor and was doing its best to digest it. There was immediate loud applause from the enthusiastic Asians, impressed with a vacuum so strong it ripped the carpet off the floor. They cheered and walked into the sales area to make a deal.

After they left, I pulled the rug aside to vacuum the powder up, but it didn't budge—it stuck like glue to the glass—a little scientific phenomenon that no one expected. We couldn't remove the static attraction from it, so for the next three days I invented more unique new vacuum demos than you can imagine.

That was one of the longest days of my life. I longed for that king bed. One of the advertisers from Eureka called me aside and said, "Don, the president of Eureka loves hockey and wants you to go with him and six others to the Blackhawk game tonight." I didn't have much choice but to say yes. So I went and there was a fine menu of fights to watch—on the ice, in the stands, or in the parking lots. Plus, 15,000 groaning fans, pucks flying around at 100 miles an hour, and beer spraying down your neck from the 6'4" gorilla sitting behind you. It went on for three hours, and I could hardly wait for it to end. Then in the last thirty seconds, Edmondton tied and the game went into overtime. It ended at midnight, and I was up again at 6 A.M. After the last day, I fired my fairy godmother

Flunking English 101

*Tailoring your message for your audience always
means better communication.*

Back in my high school teaching days, when I was attempting to teach the language to teenagers, I assumed all English was English. But during my book promotion tours in England I soon discovered that many of our "Yank" expressions were completely unknown, or caused some consternation there. On my first couple of tours they attempted to clue me in nicely.

"Mr. Aslett, you do use some words, Americanisms, we might say, that aren't known here." At first they just told me. The next trip I was immediately given a neat set of typed pages: toilets are loos, diapers are nappies, a wastepaper basket is a dustbin, a condo is a flat, etc. One prompter told me, "Don, you use one word—janitor—a lot and it just isn't used here."

That I remembered and plugged into my interview mind. The very next morning I was on the "Good Morning, England" program watched by eight million people. The Duke of Devonshire was one of their guests, a lord, a famous chef, and me, the toilet cleaner. In a lovely English accent the host introduced me and asked, "Just what do you do in America, Mr. Aslett?" Determined to avoid the word "janitor," I said, "Oh, I'm just an old scrubber from Idaho." The other guests gasped in horror and the host blanched and quickly covered the microphone. I found out later that in England a scrubber is a hooker!

Two days later I told an eager audience that what they really needed was a Doodlebug. (3M's long-handled floor cleaning tool.) Again, everyone drew back in horror—later I discovered that "doodlebug" was what the British called the whistling bombs the Germans pelted them with during World War II.

Answering questions at a rapid rate, I would describe something as "rinky dink," or "klutzy," and then throw in a few "scruds" (a Utah swear word). In an interview in Scotland, when asked how I liked the country, I made the mistake of saying "Northern England is beautiful" (which was certainly good for a few gasps). In another Scottish interview, I was telling a woman how to clean her tub and told her to "really scrub that dude down," only to be asked, in sweet Scottish brogue, "Mister Aslett, vots a 'dewed?'" I told one elegant female host of a dejunking segment I'd like to look in her drawers at home, and the studio staff came unglued and she turned red. Apparently we were each thinking of very different things.

When I arrived in St. Louis once on a book tour, the pretty 45-year-old escort Penguin had hired picked me up in her sunroofed BMW, blushing, excited, almost panting, but not for me. She had driven Kirk Douglas around for the past two days and had just dropped him off. She carried on the whole day about his robust condition for a seventy-four-year-old, and his dimpled chin. I thought I was rather dynamic, too, after all I'd cleaned 10,000 toilets and Douglas only made 90 movies. I didn't see how I could fail to impress a beautiful woman, after all, I rescued old ladies from stains, held doors open for women, ohhhed over the city's famous arch, and gave her a fancy dustcloth. She kept giving me that "Well, after Kirk…" look. "Just wait, Honey, till I'm 74. I'll have cleaned 100,000 toilets!"

Life on the front page

When dealing with the media, never pose for or say anything you wouldn't want printed!

I clicked well with the media and was featured in many full-page spreads in major newspapers and magazines, and did finally make a front page. The last night of a ten-day tour in Great Britain, a photographer from the *Weekly World News* showed up at the publisher's home to take some pictures of "America's #1 Cleaning Expert," "Just to have some on file," he said. I struck every pose imaginable to complement my cleaning message. Then he said, "Just for fun, give me a funny pose." I declined to be "silly," but he assured me that the Brits loved cutups and that a picture of me with an apron and duster would be "a riot." Reluctantly I agreed to just one shot. I put my foot on my toilet suitcase, and held the duster like a spear across my shoulder. "Now look arrogant, confident, triumphant," he said, as his Nikon clicked away.

Then I shed that silly apron and went home. About a year later I received a phone call from an anxious daughter in Alaska. "Dad, you aren't going to believe this, but you are on the front page of a supermarket rag." "You're kidding—which one?" I said. "That one that is about four grades below the *National Enquirer*," she said.

One of my staff rushed to the nearest supermarket to retrieve my latest publicity and sure enough, right at the top of the front page, big as life, there was the picture of me—apron tied around me, chin in air, and foot on toilet, beneath a big, black headline that said, "The Man Women Hate—he can clean house in 15 minutes!" (The writeup inside was even less flattering, including a headline quoting me as saying, "If it takes more than 15 minutes to tidy up your home you are a flop as a housewife.") Fifteen years later, the picture was used again, this time with the headline, "How to turn any man into a slave—it's just like training a dog." The accompanying article, among other things, advised women to withhold sex to get their men to do the cleaning. This was dismaying, but believe it or not, when we sought the source of the article, we couldn't pin it down (we wrote and called and left messages, but never got an answer).

In the eye of the beholder

We were filming on location in a home for the Discovery channel with a crew out of Canada, when the cameraman suddenly stopped and said, "Mr. Aslett, do you realize you look just like Sean Connery?" (The original James Bond.) Boy, did that make my morning! I "James Bonded" my way through the next several hours, figuring that even "the golden years" had some merits I'd missed till now. Finishing up the segment in one of my stores, they filmed me with a customer. Afterward, she picked up a bottle of my new "3 in 1 Spotter" which had a picture of me in a white sports coat on the label. She held it up and exclaimed, "Wow, Mr. Aslett, look at this, you look just like an Oompa Loompa (the diminutive workmen in *Willie Wonka and the Chocolate Factory*). I looked down at it and sure, enough, I did! (a lot more than I looked like Sean Connery). It's nice sometimes to get perspective, even if it sets you back a bit.

082

Afterword

The little business I started in an Idaho college town is now one of the top in the industry, operating in fifty states and Canada and soon headed overseas.

With the great expansion of the areas we clean and services we offer, the "experience" stories I collected over the years will soon be dwarfed by what you'd imagine and expect when servicing 400 million square feet of floor space every day. One night not long ago, for instance, a drunk drove a truck into the center of a department store we cleaned; the next night two of my 60-year-old female janitors pounced on and wrestled down a robber; the next day a police horse threw a shoe and we re-shoed the horse; the next night two of my Varsity trucks crashed in an empty parking lot—into each other! The next night one of our janitors (watching an x-rated tape in a big corporate training auditorium) forgot and left it in the VCR, and the next day the CEO, unaware, clicked it on in front of a room full of guests

Looking forward to Volume 2—there is never an uneventful day in the cleaning business.

—Don Aslett

Would you like to be in Volume 2?

Let's partner on a Volume 2 of janitor journals, the lighter and brighter side of the broom!

If you will send me your cleaning-related story or adventure (or stories you have heard from others), Marsh Creek Press, my publishing company, will edit, organize, and illustrate it along with other cleaning capers and produce another book like this, with full credit given to you and other contributors and the right to purchase books at a great price to resell, distribute, or give away to colleagues, family, and friends.

Send your stories to:

> Funny Stories
> Volume 2
> Marsh Creek Press
> PO Box 700
> Pocatello, ID 83204

Include any further explanation your story or stories may need, and an indication of whether times, places, and names can be used as supplied or need to be changed to preserve anonymity.

Other books you will enjoy

How I Swept My Way to the Top: The Don Aslett Story

If you enjoyed The Brighter Side of the Broom, you've had the appetizer. Here now is the main course: The believe it or not, start-to-finish story of the man who not only made a million scrubbing toilets, but made Americans sit up and take notice of cleaning. Full of business and personal insight, inspiration, humor, and hundreds of photos. $24.99

How to Upgrade & Motivate Your Cleaning Crews

Don shares hundreds of ways to uplift the image of "the cleaner" and motivate crews to take pride in their work. Get the benefit of more than 50 years of firsthand, front-line experience of what really works, and what doesn't when it comes to encouraging professional cleaners. $19.95

The Professional Cleaner's Personal Handbook

The most comprehensive training manual ever for the frontline cleaner. You will learn here from a master, not merely how to clean, but all the hidden and equally important "people" skills. Every crew member should have his or her own copy. $19.95

Cleaning up for a living

A complete, comprehensive, step-by-step guide to ev-ery-thing you need to know to start your own cleaning business. Cleaning is one of the easiest fields to enter—it requires little startup capital or special skills, while offering good income and growth potential and freedom of choice and operation. This book is written in a down-to-earth, lively style that makes even the most technical subject easy to grasp and understand, and it includes 34 pages of forms of all kinds you can just photocopy and use. $39.95

" My focus for years now has been on giving you more time by showing you how you can accomplish things better and faster. How to free yourself up so you can have more of what you really want out of life. My books are loaded with fresh, new, and down-to-earth solutions for getting 'it' all done, so you can move on to things that really matter to you. "

AUTOBIOGRAPHY!

BUSINESS

** Formerly *How to Have a 48-Hour Day*

MAIL your order to:
Don Aslett
PO Box 700
Pocatello ID 83204
CALL: 888-748-3535
        208-232-3535
FAX: 208-235-5481
ONLINE: www.Aslett.com

☐ Don, please put my name and the enclosed list of my friends on your mailing list for the **Clean Report** bulletin and catalog.

Broom 2008

TITLE	Retail	Qty	Amt
Barnyard to Boardroom: Business Basics	$14.95		
Clean in a Minute	$6.95		
DVD Clean in a Minute	$14.99		
Cleaning Up for a Living (Revised)	$39.95		
Clutter Free! Finally & Forever	$12.99		
Clutter's Last Stand, 2nd Edition	$9.95		
Construction Cleanup	$19.95		
CD Dejunk LIVE! *Audio CD*	$14.99		
Don Aslett's Stainbuster's Bible	$13.95		
Done! (Formerly How to Have a 48-Hour Day)	$9.95		
Do I Dust Or Vacuum First? 2nd Edition	$9.95		
For Packrats Only	$13.95		
Get Organized, Get Published	$18.99		
HELP! How to get help around the House	$9.95		
How I Swept My Way to the Top	$24.99		
How to Be #1 With Your Boss	$9.99		
How to Handle 1,000 Things at Once	$12.99		
How to Upgrade & Motivate Your Cleaning Crew	$19.95		
How to Write & Sell Your First Book	$14.95		
Is There Life After Housework? 2nd Edition	$9.95		
DVD/VHS Is There Life After Housework?	$19.95		
Make Your House Do the Housework	$19.95		
No Time To Clean! (+ free color spot chart)	$12.99		
Painting Without Fainting	$9.99		
Pet Clean-Up Made Easy, 2nd Edition	$9.95		
CD Professional Cleaner's Clip Art	$29.95		
DVD/VHS Restroom Sanitation (with Quiz Booklet)	$69.95		
Speak Up (Don's guide to public speaking)	$12.99		
The Brighter Side of the Broom	16.95		
The Cleaning Encyclopedia	$16.95		
The Office Clutter Cure, 2nd Edition	$9.95		
The Professional Cleaner's Handbook	$19.95		
Weekend Makeover (Formerly Lose 200 Lbs...)	$9.95		
Who Says It's A Woman's Job to Clean?	$6.95		
Wood Floor Care	$9.95		

Shipping: $3.25 for first book or video plus 75¢ for each additional.		
	Subtotal	
	Idaho residents only add 5% Sales Tax	
	Shipping	
	TOTAL	

☐ Check enclosed   ☐ Visa   ☐ MasterCard   ☐ Discover   ☐ AmEx

Card No. _____ CVV _____

Exp. Date_____ Phone _____

Signature X _____

Ship to:
Your Name_____

Street Address _____

City ST Zip_____

CLEANING – New Editions!

HELP! Around the House

 NEW Book!

IS THERE LIFE AFTER HOUSEWORK? — 2nd Edition

PET CLEAN-UP MADE EASY — 2nd Edition

DO I DUST OR VACUUM FIRST? — 2nd Edition

MAKE YOUR HOUSE DO THE HOUSEWORK

stain BUSTER'S BIBLE

The Guide to **HARD WOOD FLOOR** Care & Maintenance — GRANT ASLETT

DON ASLETT NO TIME TO CLEAN!

CLEAN IN A MINUTE

The **CLEANING ENCYCLOPEDIA** — Don Aslett

WHO SAYS IT'S A WOMAN'S JOB TO CLEAN? — DON ASLETT

DECLUTTERING

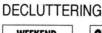 
WEEKEND MAKEOVER — 2nd Edition*

CLUTTER'S LAST STAND — 2nd Edition

THE OFFICE CLUTTER CURE — 2nd Edition

DON ASLETT'S CLUTTER FREE! Finally & Forever

For Packrats Only

* Formerly *Lose 200 Lbs. This Weekend*

VIDEOS

Don Aslett's Video Seminar Is There Life After Housework?

CLEAN IN A MINUTE

Restroom Maintenance & Sanitation *VIDEO*

AUDIO CD

DEJUNK LIVE! with DON ASLETT

CLIP ART CD

Don Aslett's Professional Cleaner's **CLIP ART**

PROFESSIONAL CLEANERS

Cleaning up for a Living — Don A. Aslett, Mark L. Browning

THE PROFESSIONAL CLEANER'S PERSONAL HANDBOOK

HOW TO UPGRADE AND MOTIVATE YOUR CLEANING CREWS

CONSTRUCTION CLEANUP

Painting without Fainting — DON ASLETT

WRITING

Get Organized, Get Published! — 225 Ways to Make Time for Success — Don Aslett and Carol Cartaino

HOW TO WRITE & SELL YOUR FIRST BOOK — Don Aslett

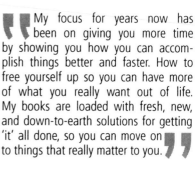
> My focus for years now has been on giving you more time by showing you how you can accomplish things better and faster. How to free yourself up so you can have more of what you really want out of life. My books are loaded with fresh, new, and down-to-earth solutions for getting 'it' all done, so you can move on to things that really matter to you.

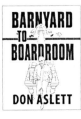

TITLE	Retail	Qty	Amt
Barnyard to Boardroom: Business Basics	$14.95		
Clean in a Minute	$6.95		
DVD Clean in a Minute	$14.99		
Cleaning Up for a Living (Revised)	$39.95		
Clutter Free! Finally & Forever	$12.99		
Clutter's Last Stand, 2nd Edition	$9.95		
Construction Cleanup	$19.95		
CD Dejunk LIVE! *Audio CD*	$14.99		
Don Aslett's Stainbuster's Bible	$13.95		
Done! (Formerly How to Have a 48-Hour Day)	$9.95		
Do I Dust Or Vacuum First? 2nd Edition	$9.95		
For Packrats Only	$13.95		
Get Organized, Get Published	$18.99		
HELP! How to get help around the House	$9.95		
How I Swept My Way to the Top	$24.99		
How to Be #1 With Your Boss	$9.99		
How to Handle 1,000 Things at Once	$12.99		
How to Upgrade & Motivate Your Cleaning Crew	$19.95		
How to Write & Sell Your First Book	$14.95		
Is There Life After Housework? 2nd Edition	$9.95		
DVD/VHS Is There Life After Housework?	$19.95		
Make Your House Do the Housework	$19.95		
No Time To Clean! (+ free color spot chart)	$12.99		
Painting Without Fainting	$9.99		
Pet Clean-Up Made Easy, 2nd Edition	$9.95		
CD Professional Cleaner's Clip Art	$29.95		
DVD/VHS Restroom Sanitation (with Quiz Booklet)	$69.95		
Speak Up (Don's guide to public speaking)	$12.99		
The Brighter Side of the Broom	16.95		
The Cleaning Encyclopedia	$16.95		
The Office Clutter Cure, 2nd Edition	$9.95		
The Professional Cleaner's Handbook	$19.95		
Weekend Makeover (Formerly Lose 200 Lbs...)	$9.95		
Who Says It's A Woman's Job to Clean?	$6.95		
Wood Floor Care	$9.95		

Shipping: $3.25 for first book or video plus 75¢ for each additional.		
	Subtotal	
Idaho residents only add 5% Sales Tax		
	Shipping	
	TOTAL	

☐ Check enclosed ☐ Visa ☐ MasterCard ☐ Discover ☐ AmEx

Card No. _____ CVV _____

Exp. Date_____ Phone _____

Signature X _____

Ship to:
Your Name_____

Street Address _____

City ST Zip_____

Printed in the United States
119339LV00003B/1-150/P